A TEXTBOOK OF

ARTIFICIAL INTELLIGENCE

(Unlocking the Secrets of AI)

Subject Code: 901 B | Skill Education

(As per Latest NEP Guidelines)

7
CBSE

Name ....
Class .... Section .... Roll No. ....
School ....
Address ....
Phone ....

Preeti Saxena

A TEXTBOOK OF

ARTIFICIAL INTELLIGENCE

(Unlocking the Secrets of AI)

Subject Code: 901 B | Skill Education

(As per Latest NEP Guidelines)

Class VII

By:

Preeti Saxena

Suvigya Saxena

S.K. KATARIA & SONS®

Educational Publishers

4885/109, Prakash Mahal, Dr. Subhash Bhargav Lane,
Opposite Delhi Medical Association, Daryaganj, New Delhi-110002 (INDIA)
Phone: +91-11-43551243; Mobile: +91-9871775858, 7678425209
e-mail: katariabook@gmail.com; katariabooks@yahoo.com
Website: www.skkatariaandsons.com

(e-books, subscriptions and bulk buying also available on our website)

Published by:

S.K. Kataria & Sons®

4885/109, Prakash Mahal, Dr. Subhash Bhargav Lane,
Opposite Delhi Medical Association, Daryaganj, New Delhi-110002 (INDIA)
Phone: +91-11-43551243; Mobile: +91-9871775858, 7678425209
e-mail: katariabook@gmail.com; katariabooks@yahoo.com
Website: www.skkatariaandsons.com

Send all correspondence to : **M/s. S.K. Kataria & Sons,** New Delhi
Email: katariabook@gmail.com

First Edition: 2025; Second Edition: 2025-2026, Third Edition: 2026-2027

ISBN: 978-81-963589-6-9

Laser Typesetting by : S.K. Computers, Delhi | Printed at: Yash Printographics, Noida

PREFACE

Artificial intelligence (AI) has emerged as a new Technology Trend. It has reshaped industries and daily life. From self-driving cars to medical diagnoses, AI's applications are boundless. This book is an effort to bring the latest technology for students as a part of vocational education mentioned in NEP(New education Policy-2020). This book has all the latest features of AI with very interesting games that helps students to understand the technology in a better way. As AI continues to advance, it promises to further enhance productivity, personalize experiences, and drive innovation, bringing a transformative change in the technology of our time.

Class 7 (Skill module 901 B) module goes ahead with a detailed sketch of domains of AI namely Data science, Natural language processing in detail and sustainability with SDGs. Students will learn the process behind the working of an Artificial Intelligence device . They will be able to correlate human intelligence with artificial intelligence and how AI has made human difficult task simpler in real life. The book has Fun.AI activity for the students to learn and explore new AI world and some interesting Scooby-Doo quest for examining AI skill.

This book has interesting videos , theoretical and objective type questions which are important for the assessment. These questions are given in the form of activity and games so that students can learn more. This book is an effort to teach and make you understand difficult topics in easy manner and simple language. Though it has been kept in mind that errors are not there but being human, even I can commit some errors. This is my request that if you come across any such problem, kindly inform me through my email katariabook@gmail.com.

Note: CBSE Vocational Education Skill based. (According to NEP-2020).

Sources: Internet and several online AI tools with games has helped us in framing our content. My thanks and gratitude to such sources.

Preeti Saxena

ACKNOWLEDGEMENTS

My first and foremost thanks to my Almighty **'Sai Ram'**. During this journey from becoming a student to a teacher and now an author, my **'Sai Ram'** was with me throughout, inspiring me always to move ahead in life. He taught me that faith and hard work can give you everything you dream of.

I am also grateful to my parents who made me a self independent person. They gave me higher education and moral values. My dad **Mr. Som Nath Gupta** and my mom **Mrs. Lajja Gupta**, taught me how to face challenges of life.

My sincere thanks to my students who believed in me and motivated me to write this book. They trusted me and guided me by giving words to my Knowledge. So I have tried my level best to share my knowledge on this subject with my students.

A special and heart filled thanks to my husband, **Mr. Sharad Saxena** and my son, **Suvigya** who compromised a lot during my journey as an author. They motivated me, trusted me and helped me in day-to-day working. I could have never, thought of writing this book without their support.

Last but not the least, I am grateful to my in-laws and friends who were constantly guiding me and giving me emotional and moral support during my work. I would also like to give my special thanks to one of my friend, **Mr. Ashish Bhargava**, who constantly motivated me to complete my work on time.

Preeti Saxena

PUBLISHER'S PREFACE

It is with immense pride and gratitude that we present this edition under the name of M/s S.K Kataria & Sons. We have recently been awarded with the **Best Publisher Award 2025 by DSBPA, Delhi.** Receiving this award reinforces our dedication to setting high standards in editorial quality, design and reader engagement.

This recognition stands as a testament to our unwavering commitment to quality, creativity and the pursuit of excellence in the world of publishing.

For us, publishing is more than producing books. It is more about nurturing ideas, empowering voices and building a bridge between esteemed authors and young readers.

Each book of our publication is a masterpiece and is driven by our passion for knowledge, innovation and literary integrity.

We extend our heartfelt gratitude to our esteemed authors, editors, designers and most importantly readers whose trust and enthusiasm continues to inspire us.

As you turn the pages of this book, we request you to share your valuable feedback with us.

Please Email us at **katariabook@gmail.com.**

With warm regards
Sanjeev Kataria

KATSON BOOKS

M/s. S.K. Kataria & Sons
New Delhi
Website: www.skkatariaandsons.com
Email: katariabook@gmail.com

WORK DETAIL

S.No.	Chapter Name	Date	Teacher's Signature

MY PERFORMANCE

Date	Text/ Exam	Marks/Grades Obtained			Highest Marks/Grade in the class	Teacher's Remarks	Parents Signature
		Theory	Practical	Total			

CONTENTS

CHAPTER 1

NAVIGATING DOMAINS OF AI & THE CORRESPONDING EVOLVING FRONTIERS

Navigating Domains of AI & the Corresponding Evolving Frontiers in Action

Scan QR Code

OBJECTIVES

TOPICS TO BE COVERED

- Introduction to domain
- Types of Domain
- Introduction to AI Domains using Applications (Data, CV & NLP)
- Emerging Frontiers
- Ethical Consideration in Various domain
- How to Be Ethical – What Can We Do?

1.1 INTRODUCTION TO DOMAIN

Artificial Intelligence quite is a revolutionary technology that has changed the thinking process of the world. AI is the creation of machines that can mimic human capabilities such as learning, reasoning, and problem-solving. From self-driving cars to personalized virtual assistants, AI's is leaving its impact by transforming the way we work, live, and interact with technology.

AI work in many areas but it is important to understand the type of work an AI machine can do in a specific area. Based on application area, we categorize AI in three domains:

1. Data Science
2. Computer Vision
3. NLP (Natural Language Processing)

Fig. 1.1

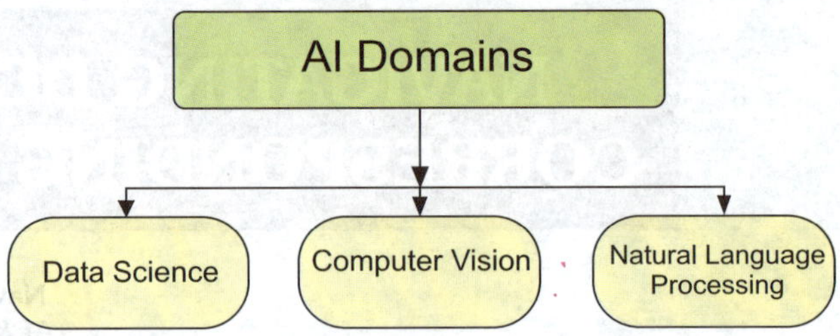

Fig. 1.2

1.2 TYPES OF DOMAIN

The domains in AI include various specialized areas wherein intelligent machines and many algorithms are developed to meet the specific challenges and applications. These domains include:

1. **Data Science:** It is a multidisciplinary field that combines mathematics, statistics, and computer science to apply machine learning algorithms to numbers, text, images, video, audio etc. in order to produce artificial intelligence (AI) systems that perform tasks like a human does. The data whether numeric, text, audio, video, image, etc. is all converted to numeric form for extraction, preparation, analysis, visualization, and also maintenance of information.

Fig. 1.3

2. **Computer Vision:** Computer Vision(CV) is the scientific technology for building artificial systems that obtain information from images, video or any other visual data. This involves several methods of acquiring, processing, analyzing, and understanding digital images, and extraction of data from the real and visual world to produce information.

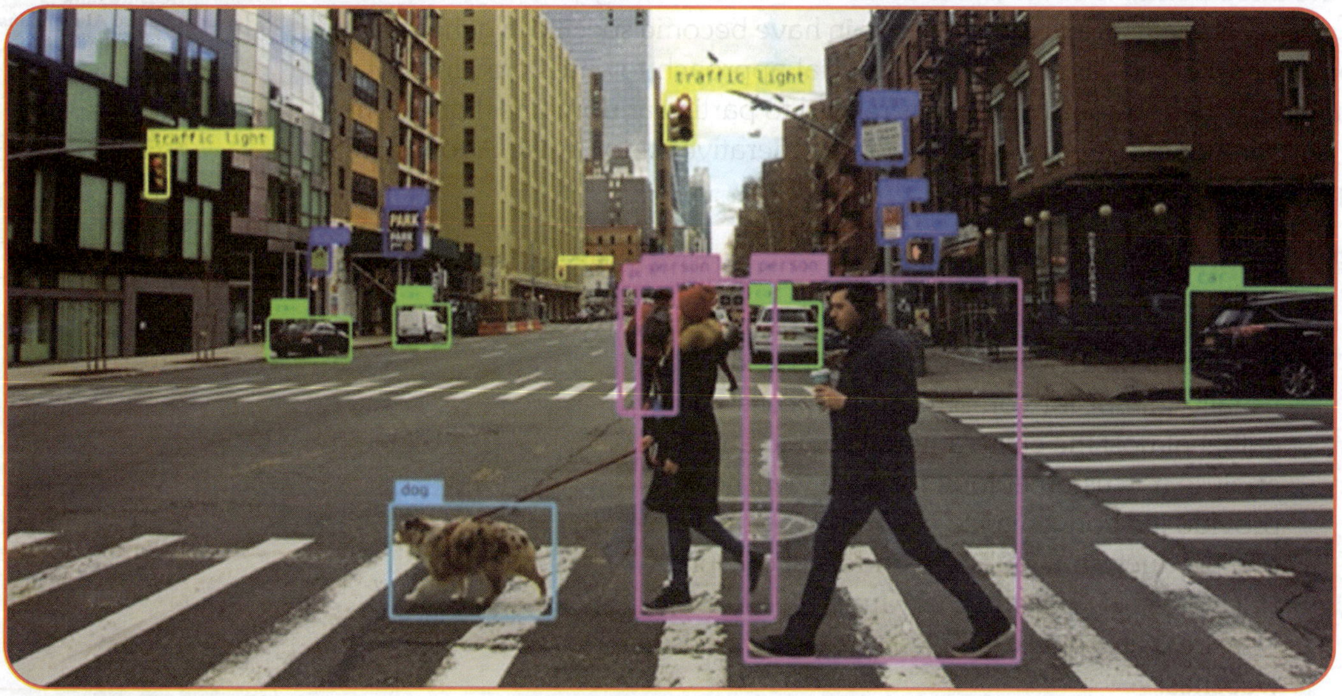

Fig. 1.4

3. **Natural Language Processing:** Natural Language Processing(NLP), is a branch of artificial intelligence that deals with the interaction between computers and humans, by using the natural language such as English, spanish, Hindi etc. In this domain , AI allows machines to understand, interpret, and generate human language. It works with text and many of the speech based data.

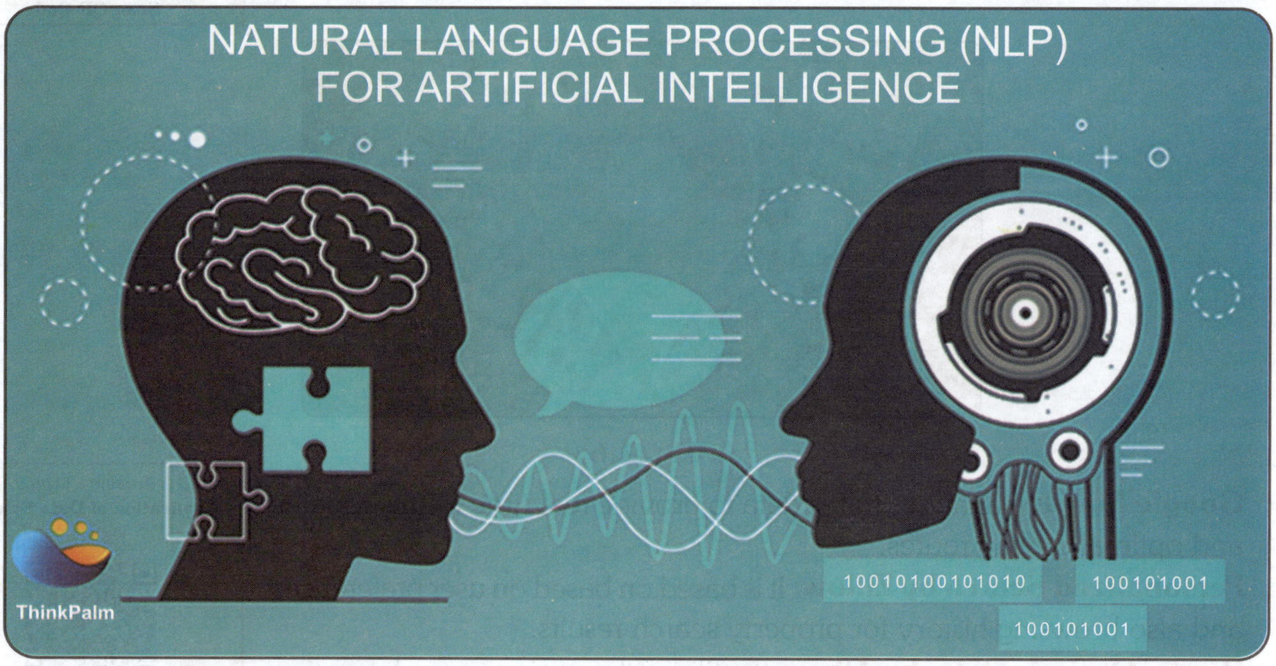

Fig. 1.5

1.3 INTRODUCTION TO AI DOMAINS USING APPLICATIONS (DATA, CV & NLP)

All the three domains cover all the areas of Artificial Intelligence. These domains cover specific fields. Now a days , domain have become specific in generative AI. Domain-specific generative AI is an special approach towards creating data by training models on specific data sets related to particular domains. For example, we can create image using text through Generative-AI tools like Adobe Firefly, Zapier, Canva, etc.

Treasure Link
Introduction to AI Domains in Action

Scan QR Code

1.3.1 Applications of Data Science

1. **Price Comparison Websites:** The websites that are being driven by lots and lots of data are usually meant for comparison purposes . They gather almost the entire amount of data and then analyse it. Customer look for such websites that provide the convenience of comparing the price of a product from multiple vendors at one place. PriceGrabber, PriceRunner, Junglee, Shopzilla, DealTime are some examples of price comparison websites.

Scooby-Doo Quest

Q. Name any two Tools that are related to Generative AI.

1. ________________
2. ________________

Answers: 1. Zapier **2.** Adobe Firefly

2. **News Feed Personalization on Facebook:** The news feed personalization help each user by analyzing their interactions, likes, dislikes, comment, etc. It also uses machine learning to detect and filter inappropriate content, ensuring community standards are thereby maintained.

Treasure Link
Understand Data Science in Action

Scan QR Code

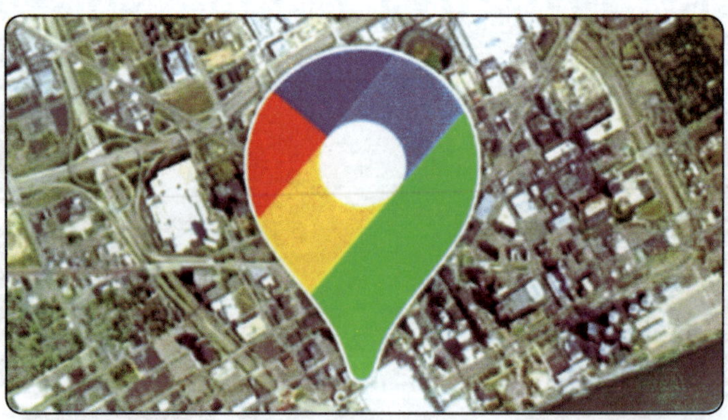

Fig. 1.6

3. **Google Maps:** It analyzes traffic data to provide real-time traffic updates and optimal driving routes.
4. **Personalized Search by Zillow:** It is based on based on user preferences and also browsing history for property search results.
5. **Route Optimization by Uber:** It utilizes data science to determine the most efficient routes for drivers, thus reducing travel time and fuel consumption.

Treasure Link
Application of Data Science in Action

Scan QR Code

FUN.AI ACTIVITY

Rock paper Scissor is an interesting game which all children love to play. There are various websites where you can play this game . Let us try two different website and explore the interesting game.

1. Visit the site: https://rockpaperscissors-ai.vercel.app/

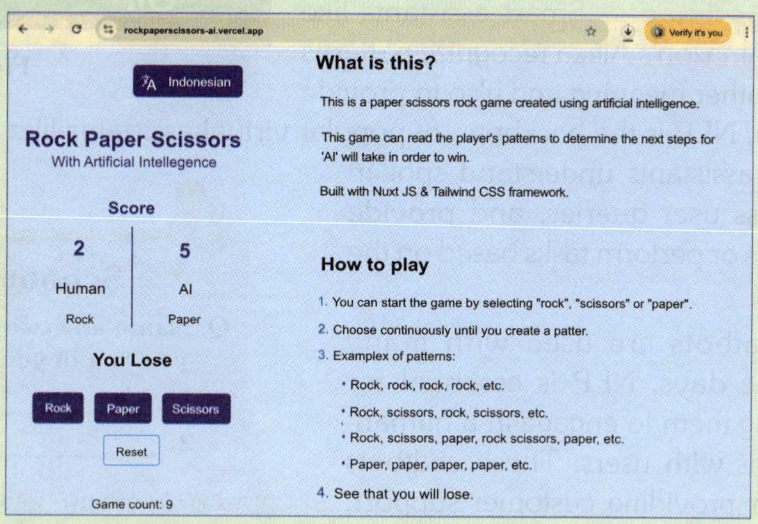

Play the interesting game of rock paper and scissor and enjoy !!!!

2. Visit the site: https://rockpaperandscissors.io/

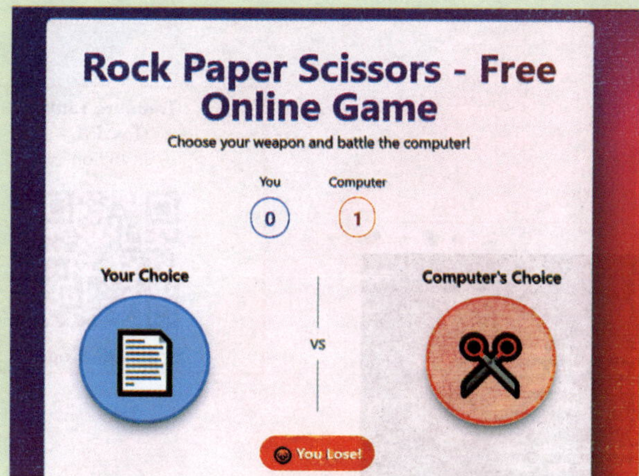

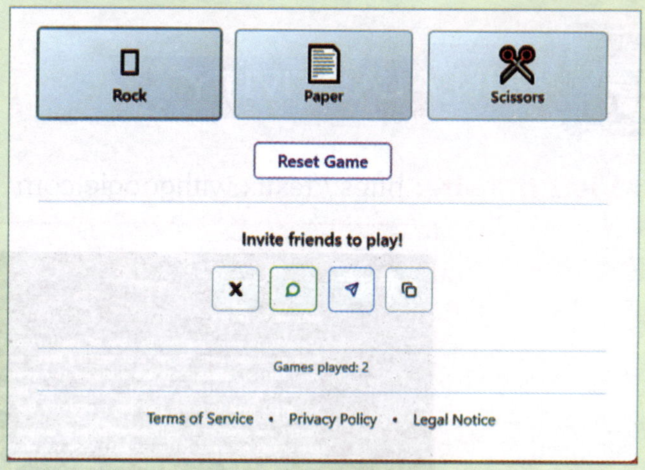

Treasure Link
Rock Paper Sensors
in Action
Scan QR Code

Treasure Link
Rpck Paper and Scissors
in Action
Scan QR Code

1.3.2 Applications of NLP

1. **Speech Recognition on Mobile Phones:** NLP controls speech recognition systems by converting spoken language into text. This technology is then used in voice-controlled devices, voice assistants, and dictation software.
2. **Language Translation on Google Translate:** NLP facilitates language translation, enabling

Treasure Link
Natural Language Processing
in Action
Scan QR Code

Treasure Link
Application of NLP
in Action
Scan QR Code

machines towards translate text from one language to another. Translation services, language learning apps, and global communication are benefitted from this application.

3. **Email Filters on Gmail:** Email filters are one of the most basic and initial applications of NLP online. It started out with various spam filters where we can mention certain words or phrases that signal a spam message.

Fig. 1.7

4. **Smart/virtual Assistants:** Smart assistants like Apple's Siri and Amazon's Alexa recognize patterns in speech, then gather meaning and also to provide a useful response. NLP is the backbone of popular virtual assistants like Siri, Alexa, and Google Assistant. These assistants understand spoken language, process user queries, and provide relevant responses or perform tasks based on the context.

5. **Chatbots:** Chatbots are used with many application these days. NLP is essential for chatbots, enabling them to engage in a human-like conversations with users. These chatbots are employed for providing customer support, helping users to ably find appropriate information, and providing personalized recommendations.

Scooby-Doo Quest

Q. Name any two Virtual assistants that you use in your daily life.

1. ______________
2. ______________

Ans. 1. Apple's Siri **2.** Amazon's Alexa

FUN.AI ACTIVITY

1. **Visit the site:** https://textfx.withgoogle.com/

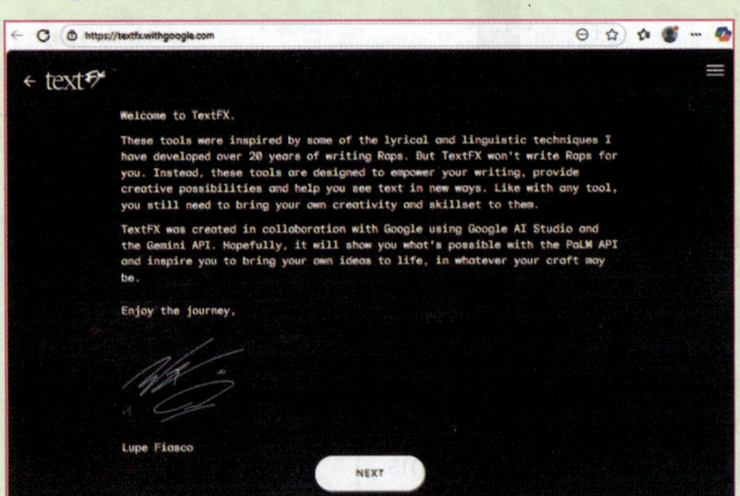

Treasure Link
TextFX in Action
Scan QR Code

2. Click next

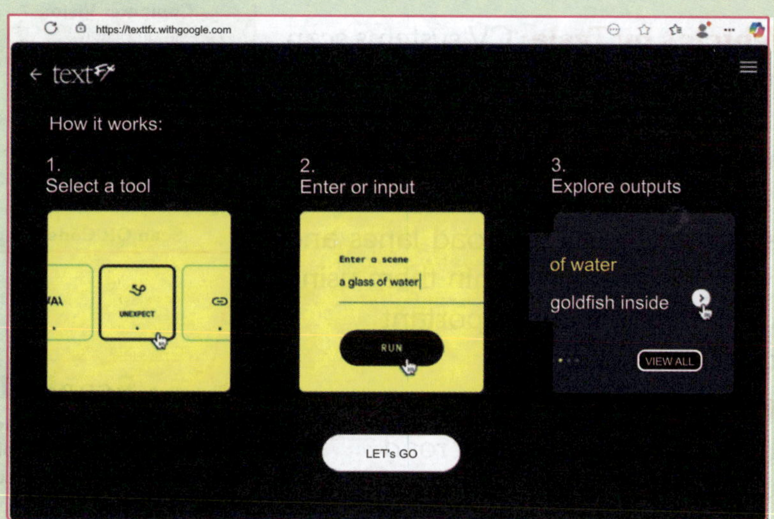

3. Click let's go.

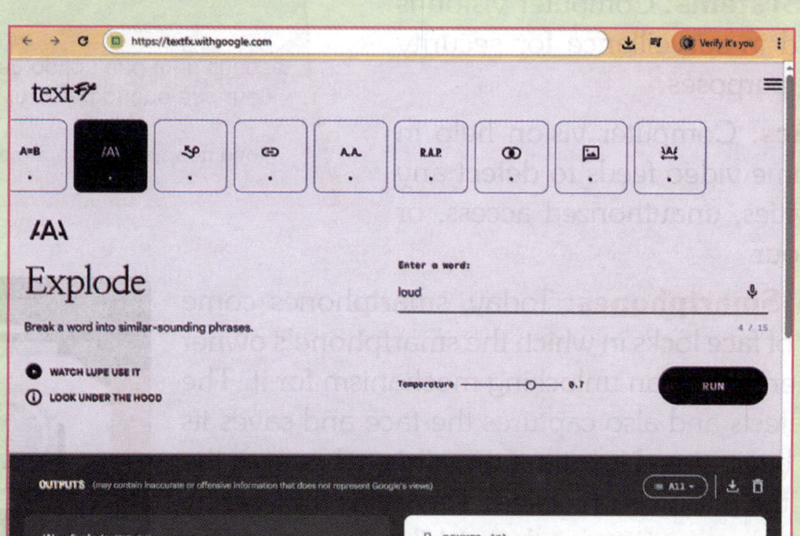

4. Click on Run

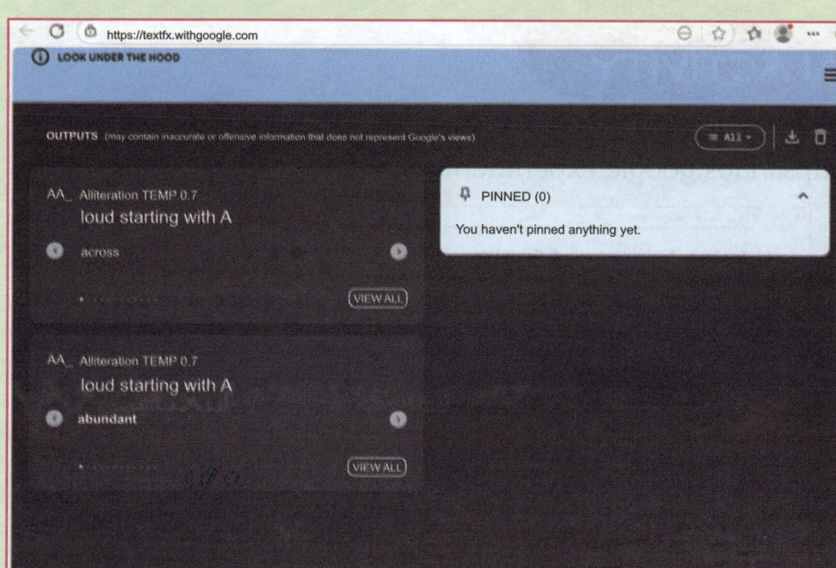

1.3.3 Applications of Computer Vision

1. **Autonomous Vehicles by Tesla:** CV systems scan live objects and fully analyse them, based on whether the car decides to keep running or to stop. Computer vision plays an important role in enabling self-driving cars to navigate, detect obstacles, and interpret traffic signs and signals. Identifying all the road lanes and maintaining the vehicle's position within them using computer vision algorithms is an important feature of autonomous vehicles.
2. **Pedestrian Detection by Tesla:** Detecting pedestrians and other hurdles on the road enhances safety for users in autonomous driving systems.
3. **Surveillance Systems:** Computer vision is extensively used in surveillance for security and monitoring purposes.
4. **Video Analytics:** Computer vision help in analysing real-time video feeds to detect any suspicious activities, unauthorized access, or unusual behaviour.
5. **Face Lock in Smartphones:** Today, smartphones come with the feature of face locks in which the smartphone's owner can set up his/her face as an unlocking mechanism for it. The front camera detects and also captures the face and saves its features during beginning. Next time onwards, whenever the features match, the phone is unlocked. This helps the user by not allowing any stranger to open the mobile.

Treasure Link
Computer Vision
in Action

Scan QR Code

Treasure Link
Applications of Computer Vision
in Action

Scan QR Code

Scooby-Doo Quest

Q. Does your father use face lock on his smart phone? Is it safe to lock your phone using face lock? Ask your father and write the process of setting face lock.

____

____

Answers: Yes, my father use face lock on phone and it is safe.
Open Settings in smart phone and then use lock screen option and then choose face lock feature

FUN.AI ACTIVITY

1. **Visit the site:** https://labs.google/experiments

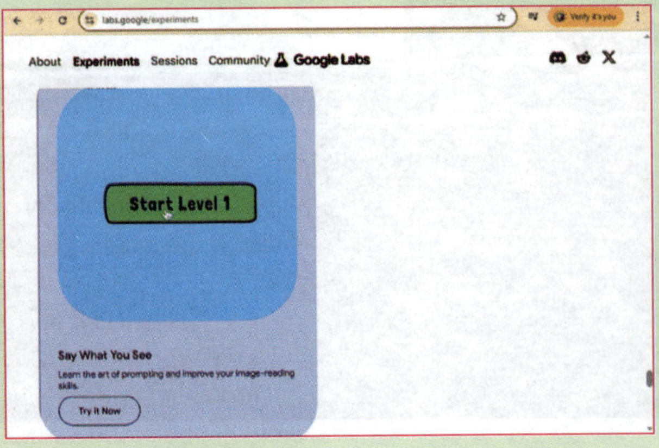

Treasure Link
Google Labs
in Action

Scan QR Code

2. Click on Try it now.

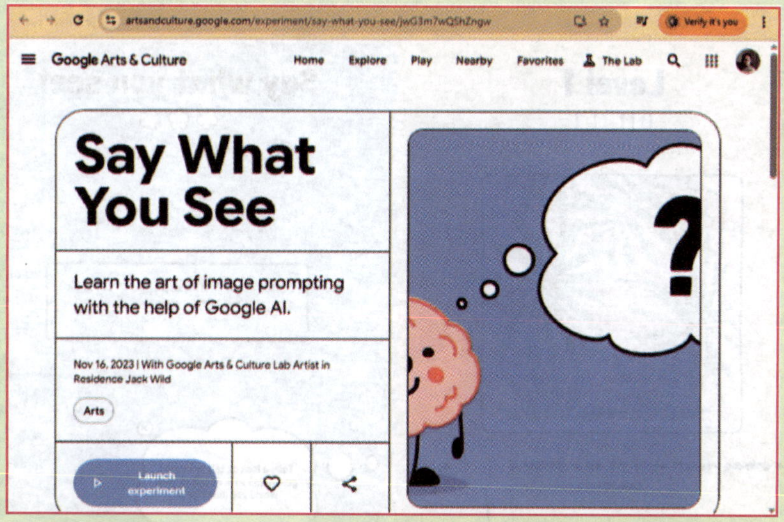

3. Click on launch Experiment.

4. Click on Start level 1

5. Click on let's begin.

6. Look at the picture and type the prompt. After you type the caption, it will generate a similar image.

1.4 EMERGING FRONTIERS

1. Generative AI

Generative AI is a type of Artificial Intelligence that can **create new things** on its own. Instead of only answering questions or following a given set of instructions, it can write stories, compose music, draw pictures, or even design new products.

- **Example:** Tools like **DALL•E** can make a painting from just a sentence, and **ChatGPT** can write essays, poems, or even computer programs.
- It helps artists, students, and companies to be more creative and save time.

FUN.AI ACTIVITY

Visit the Website: https://www.imagine.art/dashboard

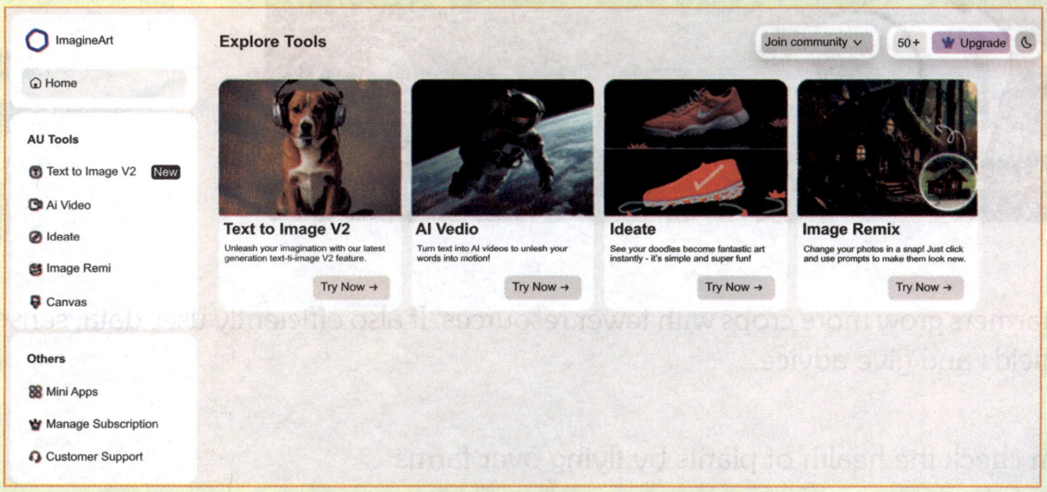

Enjoy working !!!

Treasure Link
Imagine Art
in Action

Scan QR Code

2. Healthcare AI

Healthcare AI is used in hospitals and medical research. It helps doctors and scientists to understand diseases better, treat patients faster, and even discover new medicines.

- **Examples:**
  - AI can study X-rays or MRI scans to detect diseases like cancer at an early stage.
  - AI systems can effectively recommend the best treatment for a patient.
  - Robots powered by AI can assist surgeons during operations.
- It can save lives, also reduce mistakes, and make healthcare available to more people.

3. *Education AI*

Education AI makes learning smarter and more personalized. Instead of the same lesson for everyone, AI can very well create lessons suited to each student's needs.

- **Examples:**
  - AI tutors that explain topics step by step.
  - Learning apps that adjust the level of difficulty, entirely based on the student's progress.
  - Smart classrooms with AI tools that help teachers track every student's performance.
- It makes learning easier, more fun, and accessible to children everywhere.

4. *Agriculture AI*

Agriculture AI helps farmers grow more crops with fewer resources. It also efficiently uses data, sensors, and drones to monitor fields and give advice.

- **Examples:**
  - AI drones can check the health of plants by flying over farms.
  - Sensors in the soil can measure water and nutrients and also tell the farmer when to water the crops.
  - AI systems can even predict weather changes so that farmers know the best time to plant or harvest.
- It increases food production, saves water, and supports farmers in difficult conditions.

5. Ethical AI

Ethical AI is about making sure that AI is used in a way that is fair, safe, and responsible. Since AI is very powerful, it must not be misused or cause any unforeseen harm.

- **Examples:**
  - AI should not be biased (for example, treating one group of people unfairly).
  - AI systems must protect people's privacy and not leak personal information.
  - AI should be designed to help humans, not only to replace or harm them.
- It ensures AI builds a better and fairer world for everyone.

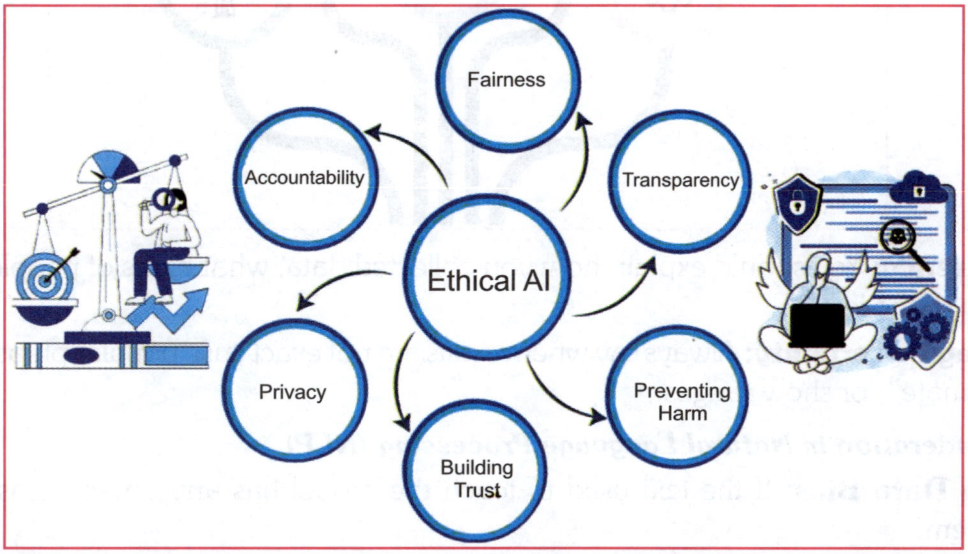

1.5 ETHICAL CONSIDERATION IN VARIOUS DOMAIN

Ethics means doing what is right. When we use data, computers, and smart programs (AI), we need to make sure they are fair, honest, and don't hurt people.

Some technical terms that are associated with ethical consideration:

- **Bias:** When something is unfair in a way that always helps one group more than others.
- **Privacy:** Keeping someone's personal information secret so others can't misuse it.
- **Consent:** Taking Permission for letting someone know what you will do with their data/images and only when they they agree.
- **Explainability:** Being able to show why a model made a decision, in a way people can understand.

1. Ethical Consideration in Statistical Data

- **Sampling Bias:** If the sample is not representative, results can be unfair.

  Example: If you survey only students who come early to school, you miss opinions of any of the latecomers.
- **Accuracy & Measurement Error:** If tools or questions are unclear, data can be wrong or misleading.
- **Privacy & Confidentiality:** If you collect personal info (name, address, health), you must keep it safe and secret.

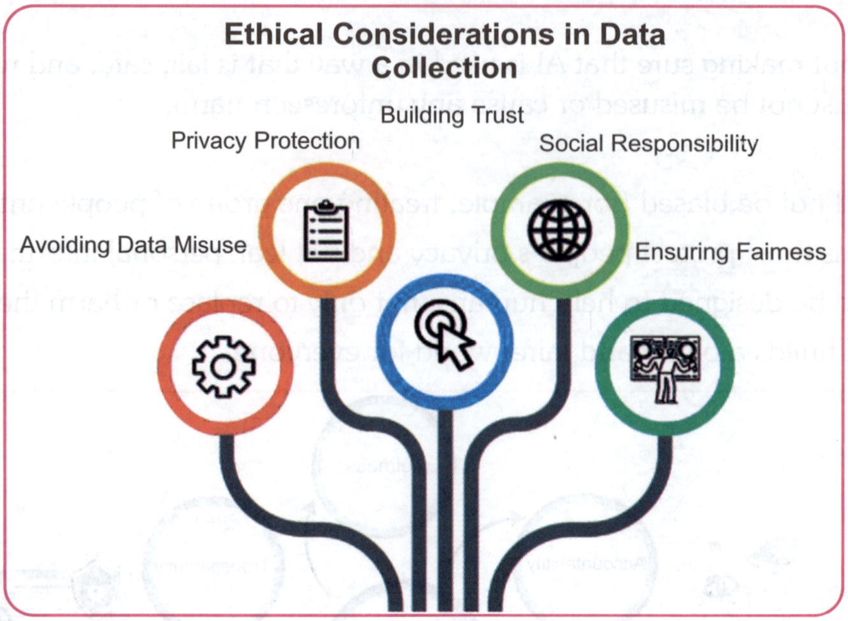

- **Transparency:** You should explain how you collected data, what kinds of people were included, what you didn't know.
- **Reporting Uncertainty:** Always say when results are not exact ; use popular phrases like "maybe", "approximate", or show ranges.

2. Ethical Consideration in Natural Language Processing (NLP)

- **Training Data Bias:** If the text used to teach the model has any unfair ideas, the model will repeat them.
- **Language Variation:** People speak in different dialects, accents or even languages. A model trained only on a few kinds might not understand everyone well.
- **Explainability:** If a model gives an answer, we should try to know why it gave that paranswer.
- **Privacy of Text:** If someone writes something private (chat, diary, etc.), using it without permission is wrong.
- **Misinformation Risk:** NLP models might generate wrong facts or misleading statements.

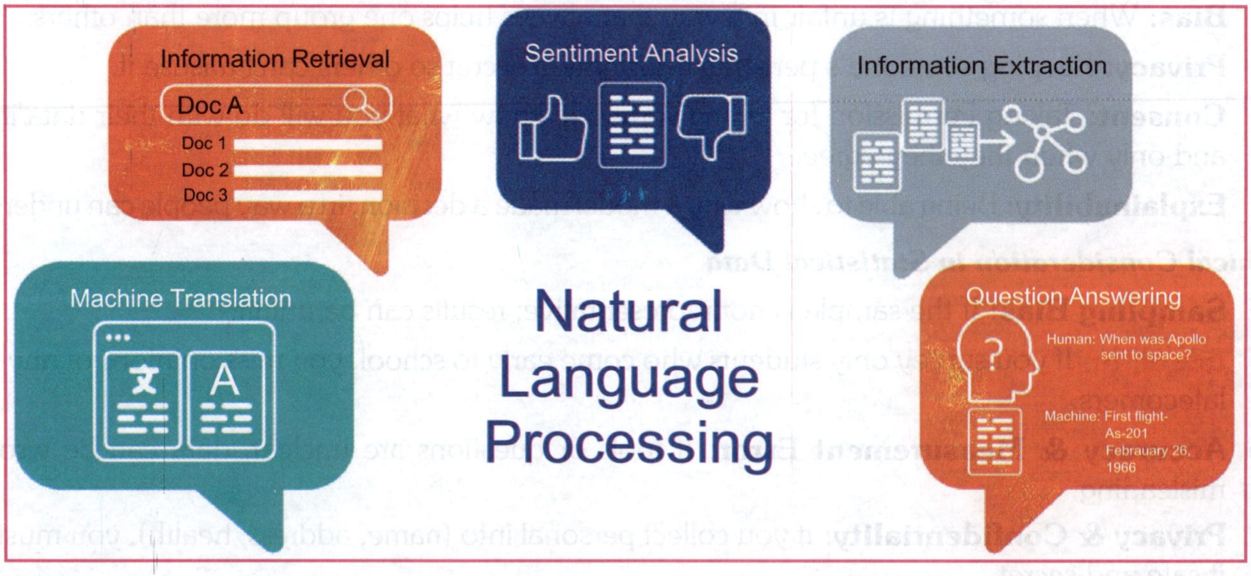

3. Ethical Consideration in Computer Vision

- **Dataset Imbalance/Skew:** If there are many pictures of some skin tones, or many of one gender and very few of others, the model may work better for the groups with many examples.
- **Consent & Privacy:** If you use images or video of people, they should totally agree. Otherwise it's unfair and possibly violates their rights.

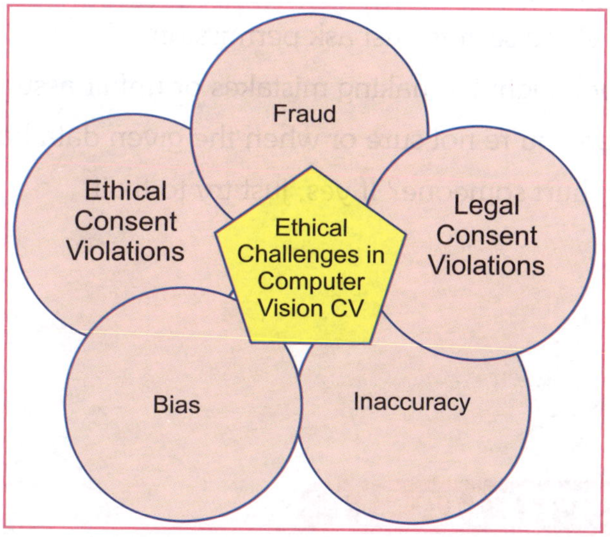

- **Misclassification:** The model might identify someone wrongly (for example, identifying gender or person incorrectly) – that can hurt people.
- **Surveillance Risk:** Using cameras and also recognition without consent can violate privacy.
- **Stereotyping:** The model might reinforce stereotypes (e.g., associating certain jobs with one gender because of biased data).

FUN.AI ACTIVITY

Treasure Link
Imagine Art
in Action

Scan QR Code

A game that gives you increasingly absurd trolley problems. Help humanity solve the philosophy by particularly solving all the trolley problems.

Visit the Link: https://neal.fun/absurd-trolley-problems/

Play this game and Enjoy !!

1.6 HOW TO BE ETHICAL – WHAT CAN WE DO?

Here are some ideas students can think about to keep things fair and safe:

- **Ask Questions:** Who collected the data? Whose voices are actually missing?
- Include many kinds of people when you collect data or images.
- Protect privacy: don't share secrets; just ask permission.
- Always check if the tool might be making mistakes or unfair assumptions.
- Be honest: admit when you're not sure or when the given data has limits.
- Think: Could this tool hurt someone? If yes, just try to fix it.

LET'S REHASH

1. **Artificial Intelligence (AI)** involves the creation of machines that can mimic human capabilities such as learning, reasoning, and problem-solving.
2. AI has transformed how we work, live, and interact with technology, within the given applications ranging from self-driving cars to personalized virtual assistants.
3. AI is divided into three main domains based on application areas: **Data Science**, **Computer Vision**, and **Natural Language Processing (NLP)**.
4. **Data Science** is a multidisciplinary field that actually applies machine learning algorithms to various forms of data, such as numbers, text, images, video, and audio, to create AI systems.
5. In Data Science, all forms of data are converted into numeric form for extraction, analysis and also all visualization
6. **Computer Vision (CV)** is a scientific technology that builds systems capable of obtaining and thereby processing information from images and visual data.
7. Computer Vision involves acquiring, processing, and analyzing digital images in order to extract useful information from the real world.
8. **Natural Language Processing (NLP)** is a branch of AI focused on the interaction between computers and humans , by using natural language, such as text and speech.
9. NLP enables machines to understand, interpret, and generate human language, facilitating applications such as speech recognition, language translation, and also chatbots.
10. The three AI domains cover all aspects of artificial intelligence, and domain-specific generative AI focuses on training models using data specific that is to particular domains.
11. **Data Science Applications** include price comparison websites, news feed personalization on social media, Google Maps for all the real-time traffic updates, personalized property search results, and Uber's route optimization.

12. **Price Comparison Websites** use large datasets to allow users to compare the prices of products from different vendors at one given location.
13. **Facebook's News Feed Personalization** utilizes user interactions and machine learning to tailor content and also filter inappropriate posts.
14. **Google Maps** applies Data Science to analyze traffic data and provide optimal driving routes in real time.
15. **NLP Applications** include speech recognition, language translation, email filters, virtual assistants, and chatbots, that help machines engage in human-like conversations.
16. **Speech Recognition** converts spoken language into text and is used in devices such as smartphones and virtual assistants.
17. **Computer Vision Applications** include autonomous vehicles, pedestrian detection, surveillance systems, video analytics, and also much of the face recognition for smartphone locks.
18. **Autonomous Vehicles** like those by Tesla rely on Computer Vision to detect obstacles, identify road signs, and ensure safe navigation.
19. **Face Lock** technology in smartphones uses Computer Vision to scan and can very well recognize a user's face for secure unlocking.
20. **Generative AI** is a specialized approach that creates new data by training models on specific datasets, such as generating images from any text by using tools like Adobe Firefly or Canva.

To Solve Multiple Choice Questions Online

Scan QR Code and Check Your Score

EXERCISE

A. Multiple Choice Questions with Answers

1. **What is Artificial Intelligence (AI)?**
   (a) The ability to create complex programs
   (b) Machines that truly mimic human capabilities
   (c) The process of converting data into information
   (d) A new programming language

2. **Which of the following is clearly a domain of AI?**
   (a) Mechanical Engineering (b) Data Science
   (c) Electrical Engineering (d) Biology

3. Which AI domain generally deals with images and video data?

(a) Natural Language Processing (NLP) (b) Data Science

(c) Computer Vision (d) Cloud Computing

4. What does NLP stand for?

(a) Neural Learning Processing (b) Natural Language Programming

(c) Natural Language Processing (d) Network Language Protocol

5. Which of these is an appropriate application of Data Science?

(a) Face Lock in Smartphones (b) Google Maps

(c) Speech Recognition (d) Chatbots

6. Which of the following is an apt example of a Price Comparison website?

(a) Siri (b) Shopzilla

(c) Facebook (d) Google Translate

7. What is an example of the Natural Language Processing application?

(a) Autonomous vehicles (b) Pedestrian detection

(c) Language translation (d) Surveillance systems

8. Which application optimally uses data to provide real-time traffic updates?

(a) Google Maps (b) Uber

(c) Gmail (d) Tesla

9. Which AI domain actually helps in analyzing real-time video feeds?

(a) Data Science (b) Computer Vision

(c) NLP (d) None of the above

10. Which company uses the principles of Computer Vision for autonomous vehicles?

(a) Google (b) Apple

(c) Tesla (d) Amazon

11. Which technology is the most common backbone of virtual assistants like Siri and Alexa?

(a) Data Science (b) Computer Vision

(c) NLP (d) Surveillance Systems

12. Which AI domain is generally involved in creating artificial systems from visual data?

(a) NLP (b) Computer Vision

(c) Machine Learning (d) Neural Networks

13. What is an application of NLP on Gmail?

(a) Route optimization (b) Email filters

(c) Surveillance app (d) Face lock

14. Which AI domain is commonly used to create data from specific datasets in Generative AI?

(a) Data Science (b) Computer Vision
(c) NLP (d) All of the above

15. What is the goal of the Natural Language Processing?

(a) Generate images (b) Understand and generate human language
(c) Analyze video feeds (d) Optimize routes for drivers

16. What is the most common application of Computer Vision in smartphones?

(a) Chatbots (b) Face lock
(c) Route optimization (d) Price comparison

17. Which AI domain mostly involves the extraction of information from real-world visual data?

(a) NLP (b) Data Science
(c) Computer Vision (d) None of the above

18. Which AI domain enables all machines to translate text from one language to another?

(a) NLP (b) Data Science
(c) Computer Vision (d) Machine Learning

19. Which application clearly helps optimize routes for Uber drivers?

(a) Speech recognition (b) Google Maps
(c) Route optimization (d) Personalized search

20. Which of these is an apt example of speech recognition?

(a) Tesla (b) Google Translate
(c) Siri (d) Uber

ANSWERS

1.	(b)	2.	(b)	3.	(c)	4.	(c)	5.	(b)
6.	(b)	7.	(c)	8.	(a)	9.	(b)	10.	(c)
11.	(c)	12.	(b)	13.	(b)	14.	(d)	15.	(b)
16.	(b)	17.	(c)	18.	(a)	19.	(c)	20.	(c)

B. Fill in the Blanks with Answers

1. AI is the creation of machines that can fully mimic human capabilities such as ________, reasoning, and problem-solving.

Ans. Human

2. The 3 core domains of AI are Data Science, Computer Vision, and ________.

Ans. Natural Language Processing (NLP)

3. ________ is a branch of AI that usually deals with interpreting and generating human language.

Ans. NLP

4. Computer Vision is primarily concerned with extracting relevant information from ________.

Ans. images and video

5. ________ websites allow all users to compare prices of products across different vendors.

Ans. Price Comparison

6. One example of the AI tool, in autonomous vehicles is ________, which uses Computer Vision.

Ans. Tesla

7. Machine learning algorithms are commonly used in ________ to analyze large datasets.

Ans. Data Science

8. NLP is essential for all smart virtual assistants like ________ and Alexa.

Ans. Siri

9. Google Maps uses data to generally provide real-time ________ updates.

Ans. traffic

10. ________ are basic applications of the NLP for sorting and managing emails.

Ans. Email filters

11. ________ helps to ably detect pedestrians in autonomous driving systems.

Ans. Computer Vision

12. ________ AI uses all specific datasets to create new data.

Ans. Generative

13. Face lock in smartphones is an example of ________ application.

Ans. Computer Vision

14. ________ helps Uber drivers to reduce their travel time by finding efficient routes.

Ans. Route optimization

15. ________ in the NLP allows machines to translate from one language to another.

Ans. Language translation

C. Short Questions with Answers

1. What is Artificial Intelligence (AI)?

Ans. AI is the creation/byproduct of machines that can mimic human abilities such as learning, reasoning, and problem-solving.

2. Name the three domains of AI.

Ans. Data Science, Computer Vision, and the Natural Language Processing (NLP).

3. What is the key role of Data Science in AI?

Ans. Data Science involves applying machine learning algorithms to data for tasks like analysis, visualization, and information extraction.

4. What is defined as Computer Vision?

Ans. Computer Vision is a technology that allows machines to obtain and process visual data from images and videos.

5. What is the purpose of the Natural Language Processing?

Ans. NLP allows machines to understand, interpret, and generate human language in a way that is useful for various applications.

6. Give one relevant example of an application of Data Science.

Ans. Google Maps, which uses data to provide real-time traffic updates.

7. What is actually Generative AI?

Ans. Generative AI is a method for creating new data by training models on specific datasets related to particular domains.

8. How does the NLP benefit virtual assistants?

Ans. NLP allows virtual assistants like Siri and Alexa to understand and respond to spoken commands from users.

9. What role does Computer Vision play in autonomous vehicles?

Ans. Computer Vision ably helps vehicles detect obstacles, recognize road signs, and interpret traffic signals for safe driving.

10. What is speech recognition in the context of NLP?

Ans. Speech recognition involves converting spoken language into text towards processing in applications like virtual assistants and voice-controlled devices.

ACTIVITY-BASED QUESTIONS

1. **Activity:** Create a drawing using a combination of generative AI tools like Adobe Firefly or Canva on "Social media".
2. **Activity:** Choose one application of the NLP (such as a chatbot or virtual assistant) and create a presentation explaining how it works and what technologies are used.
3. **Activity:** Create a drawing using a combination of generative AI tools like Adobe Firefly or Canva on the theme "Social Media".

TEACHER'S NOTES

ACTIVITY

Create a drawing using a combination of generative AI tools like **Adobe Firefly** or **Canva** on the theme "Social Media".

EXPLANATION

Students explore creativity using AI design tools to understand how **Generative AI** produces original outputs. Encourage discussion on responsible AI use and creativity ethics.

CHAPTER

2

DATA SCIENCE IN AI

Real Life Applications of Data Science
in Action

Scan QR Code

OBJECTIVES

TOPICS TO BE COVERED

- Introduction
- Data and its Types
- Big Data
- Data Science
- Importance of Data Science in AI
- Data Science Games

2.1 INTRODUCTION

Artificial Intelligence (AI) is relatively a new and a revolutionary field where we make machines smart enough to do tasks that usually need human brains. One of the key parts of AI is Data Science, that involves using data (lots of information) to learn things and make smart decisions. In this chapter, we'll explore how data is important for AI, the different types of data, and also what data science is all about.

Data Science is like a big puzzle wherein we use math, computer science, and our knowledge of the world to figure out how to use data to make smart choices. It's super important for making AI systems work well.

2.2 DATA AND ITS TYPES

Data is information we collect from different sources. It's like the building blocks for AI. Data can come from many places like sensors, websites, or even your social media posts. There are many different types of data, each with its own features. The data can be in any form like text, numbers, video, audio, animation, etc.:

1. **Structured Data:** When the data we receive from various sources is organized such that it is easy to search and sort the data for analysing purpose, it is known as the complete structured data. For Examples, data stored in spreadsheets (like Excel), databases. It becomes easy to store and analyze such data by using regular tools.

2. **Unstructured Data:** When the data we receive from various sources is not organised in a given format and it is very difficult to sort or search the data for analysing purpose, it is thereby known as unstructured data. For Examples: Text messages on various apps, photos, videos, social media posts, etc. To analyse such data ,we need special tools.

Treasure Link
Structured vs Unstructured Data
in Action

Scan QR Code

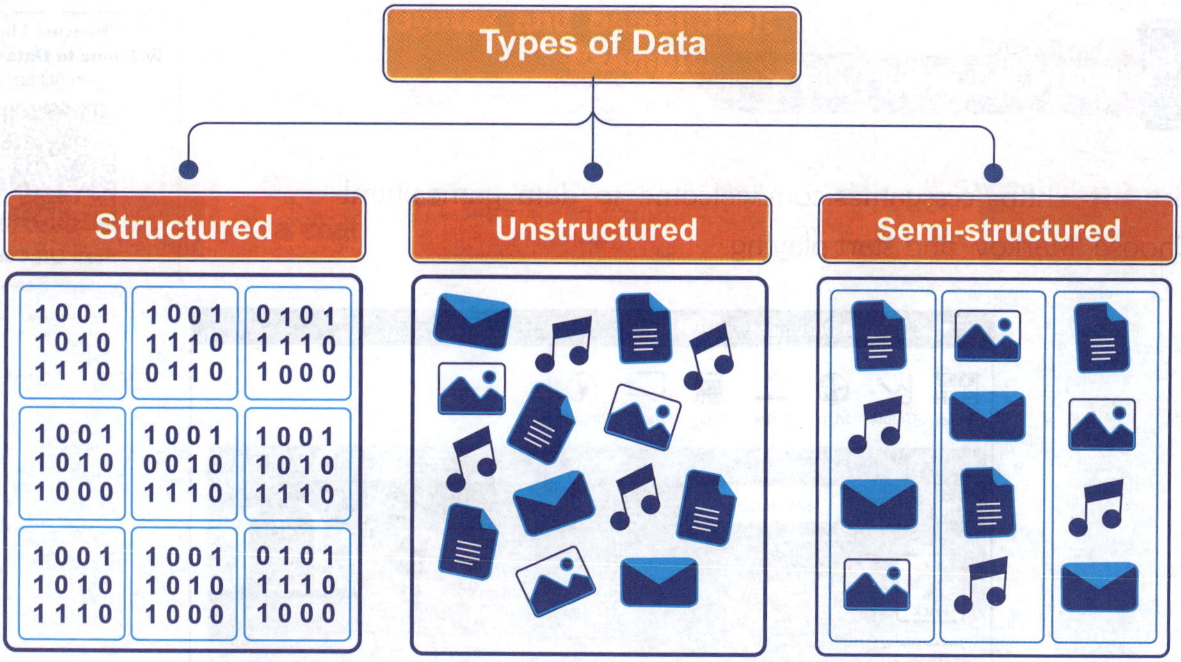

3. **Semi-structured Data:** When the data we receive from various sources is nor completely structured and nor unstructured, it comes in the category of semi-structured data. For instance; Emails, JSON files, XML files. The semi-structured data is more flexible than structured data but needs special tools to understand.

2.3 BIG DATA

In real life, large sets of data is collected from different sources and which is of different types is known as big data. Data from all of the social media platforms, sensors, scientific experiments is collected for doing analysis. It is difficult to handle this data and require special techniques and tools for analysing it because of its size and complexity.

Treasure Link
Big data in Action
Scan QR Code

2.4 DATA SCIENCE

Data science is all about using real life data to analyse and learn things for making smart decisions. It involves collecting, cleaning, exploring, analyzing, and by also optimally visualizing data. To analyse data, we need to follow a proper process. In this process, first the data is collected, then errors are corrected in data cleaning. Then we explore the data, analyse it and check the trends or pattern by visualizing it. After this, the computer learns from the data thereby, for making decision and finally we interpret the data by making right decision.

Scooby-Doo Quest

Q. Identify whether the given examples belong to structured, unstructured and semi-structured data.

1. XML files: ____________
2. Videos on social media: ____________
3. Excel file: ____________

Answers: 1. Semi-structured Data 2. Unstructured Data 3. Structured Data

FUN.AI ACTIVITY

Treasure Link
Welcome to Data Games
in Action
Scan QR Code

Visit the Site: http://ccssgames.com/welcome_to_data_games.html

1. Choose 'Markov' and start playing.

2. Choose 'Shuffleboard' and play the game.
   See how data science helps us in these games.

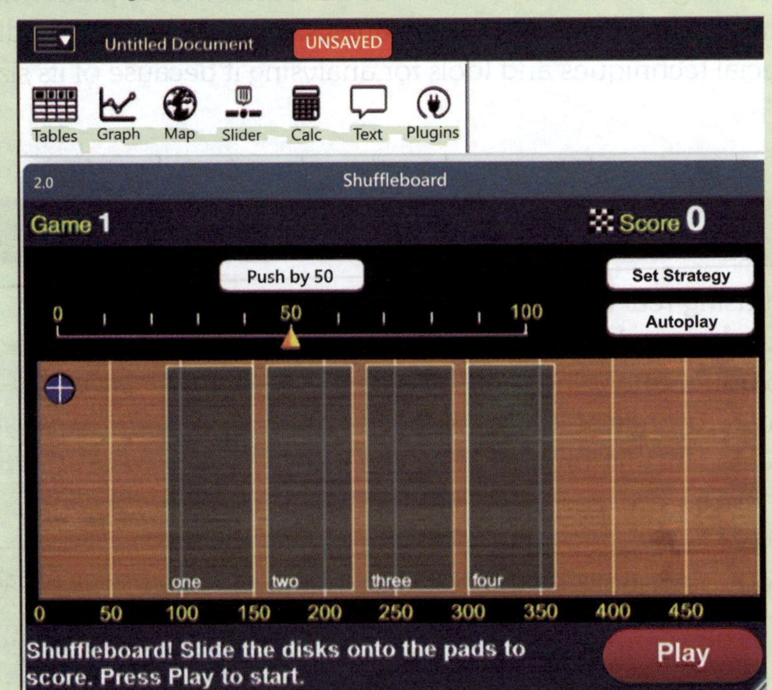

3. Choose the strategy and then click the push by 50 button to adjust the parameter according to your requirement. Then Click on Play.

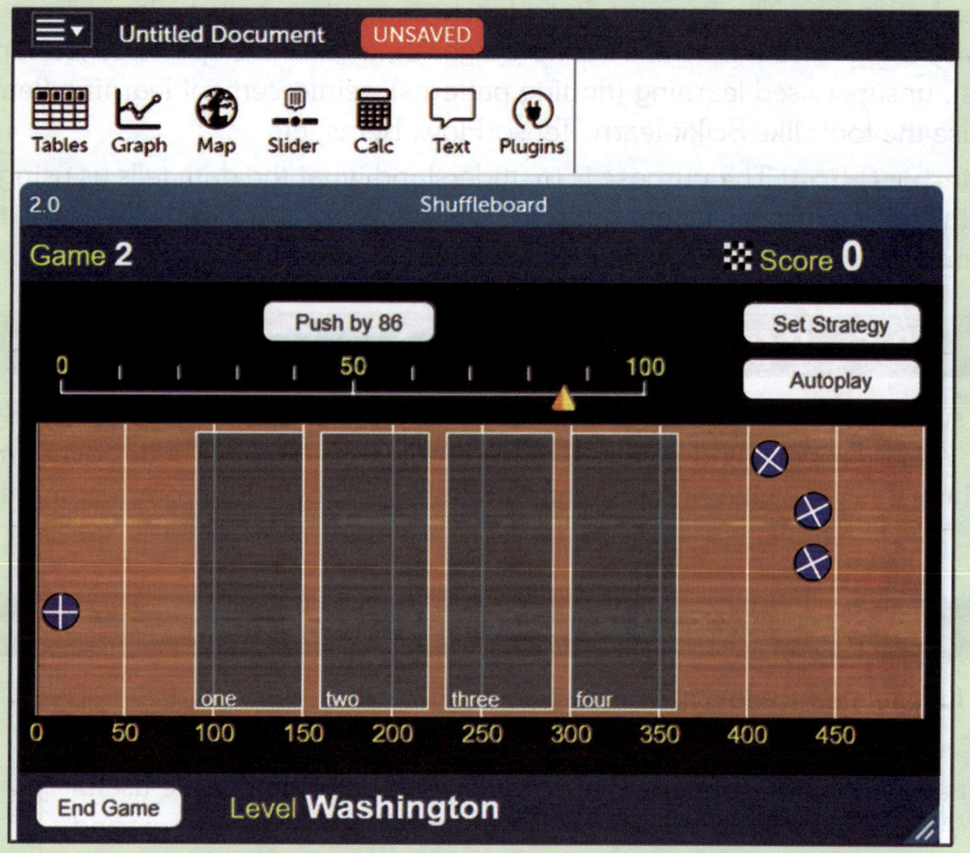

2.4.1 Key Components of Data Science

1. **Data Collection:** The purpose is to actually gather information from different places through surveys, sensors, scraping information from websites. The tools used here are Google Forms, web scraping tools, etc.
2. **Data Cleaning:** The purpose is fixing errors in the data and making it neat. In this sheer process, we remove missing or duplicate data and correct the mistakes by using various tools like Pandas (a Python tool), OpenRefine.
3. **Data Exploration:** The purpose is to know the data by looking at it closely by using charts and graphs to see what the data actually looks like. We can use the tools like matplotlib, Seaborn, Tableau, etc.
4. **Data Analysis:** The purpose is to use math and computers to find patterns and insights in the data by testing ideas, finding relationships between data points. We can also use tools like Scikit-learn (a Python tool), R, SAS.
5. **Data Visualization:** The purpose is to make the pictures (charts and graphs) to show what the data means by creating visual stories with data. It is also done by carefully using data storytelling. The tools that can be used are matplotlib, Seaborn, Tableau, Power BI.

Scooby-Doo Quest

Q. Identify the tool name associated with the component of data science:

1. Power BI: ____________
2. SAS ____________
3. Seaborn: ____________
4. Open Refine: ____________
5. Keras: ____________

Answers: 1. Data Visualization 2. Data analysis 3. Data Exploration and Visualization 4. Data Cleaning 5. Machine learning

6. **Machine Learning:** The purpose is to teach computers how to learn from data and make decisions by using various machine learning algorithms such as Supervised learning (teaching with examples), unsupervised learning (finding patterns), reinforcement learning (learning by doing). We can use the tools like Scikit-learn, TensorFlow, Keras, etc.
7. **Data Interpretation:** The purpose is to understand what the data tells us using the information by combining data insights within our knowledge base of the world. The tools that can be used are Presentation software, business intelligence tools, etc.

2.5 IMPORTANCE OF DATA SCIENCE IN AI

Data science is super important for AI because it helps machines learn from data. By looking at lots and lots of data, AI systems can find patterns, make predictions, and get better over time. This learning process is called machine learning and it's what makes AI so powerful, from recommending movies to self-driving cars.

2.6 DATA SCIENCE GAMES

Games that are fully related to data science are:

Game 1: CodeCombat: A coding game where you write code to control characters in a fantasy world. It supports Python and JavaScript, both quite useful for data science. Although more focused on programming, it develops the logic and problem-solving skills necessary for data science.

Treasure Link
CodeCombat
in Action
Scan QR Code

Step 1: Click: https://codecombat.com/play/junior

Step 2: Choose the category.

Step 3: Click on Play codecombat junior and then on the below screen, just click on the top left corner.

Step 4: Click on Play.

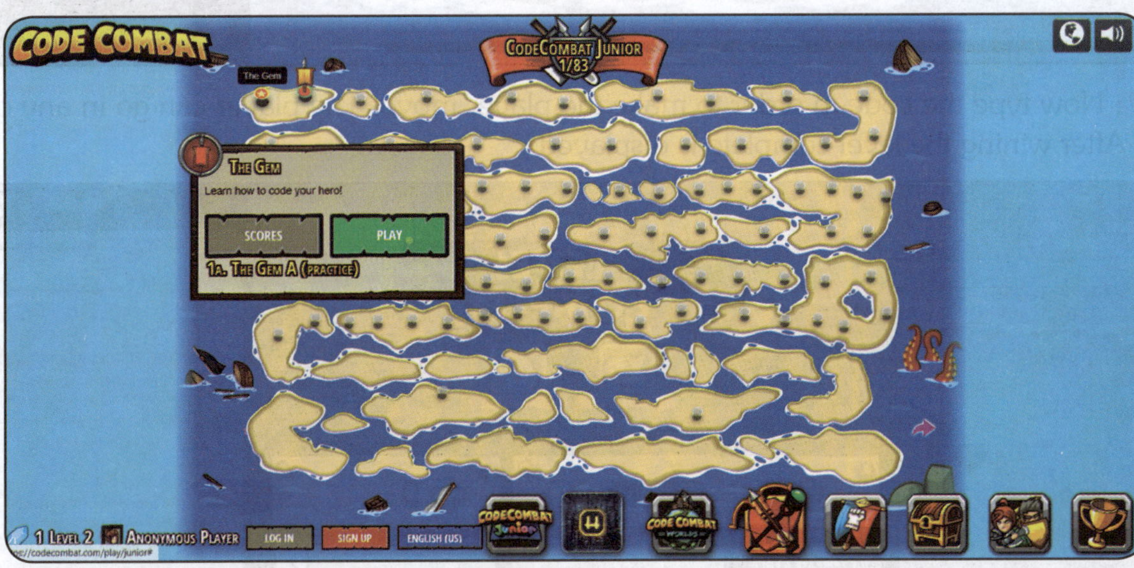

Step 5: The following screens then appears.

Step 6: Immediately the screen changes as shown below after choosing the player.

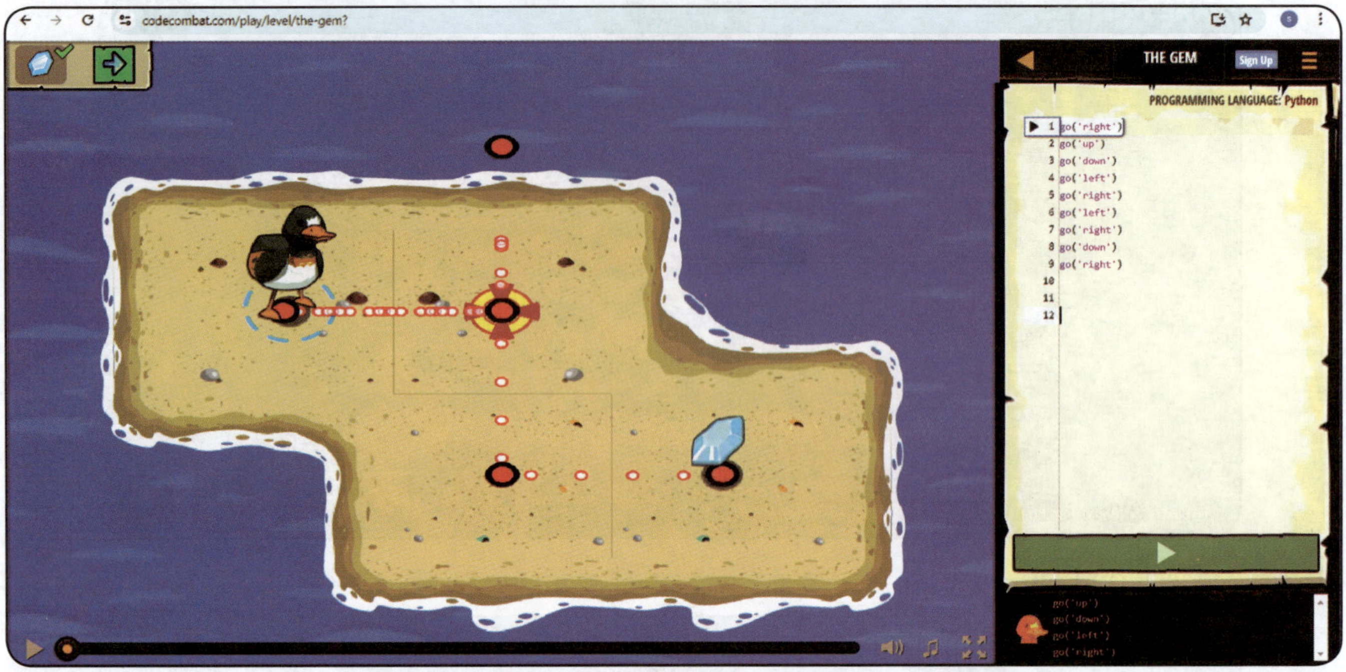

Step 7: Now type the code in order to make the player move. The player can go in any of the four directions. After wining the level complete is displayed.

Game 2: Visit the Site: https://www.firebolt.io/big-data-game

Step 1: Click on the Link: https://www.firebolt.io/big-data-game and scroll down after accepting the cookies.

Treasure Link
Game 2
in Action

Scan QR Code

Step 2: Using navigation button, move the data engineer ahead.

Step 3: Let the engineer fill up the gaps by dragging the boxes.

Step 4: Let the engineer cross the pipeline.

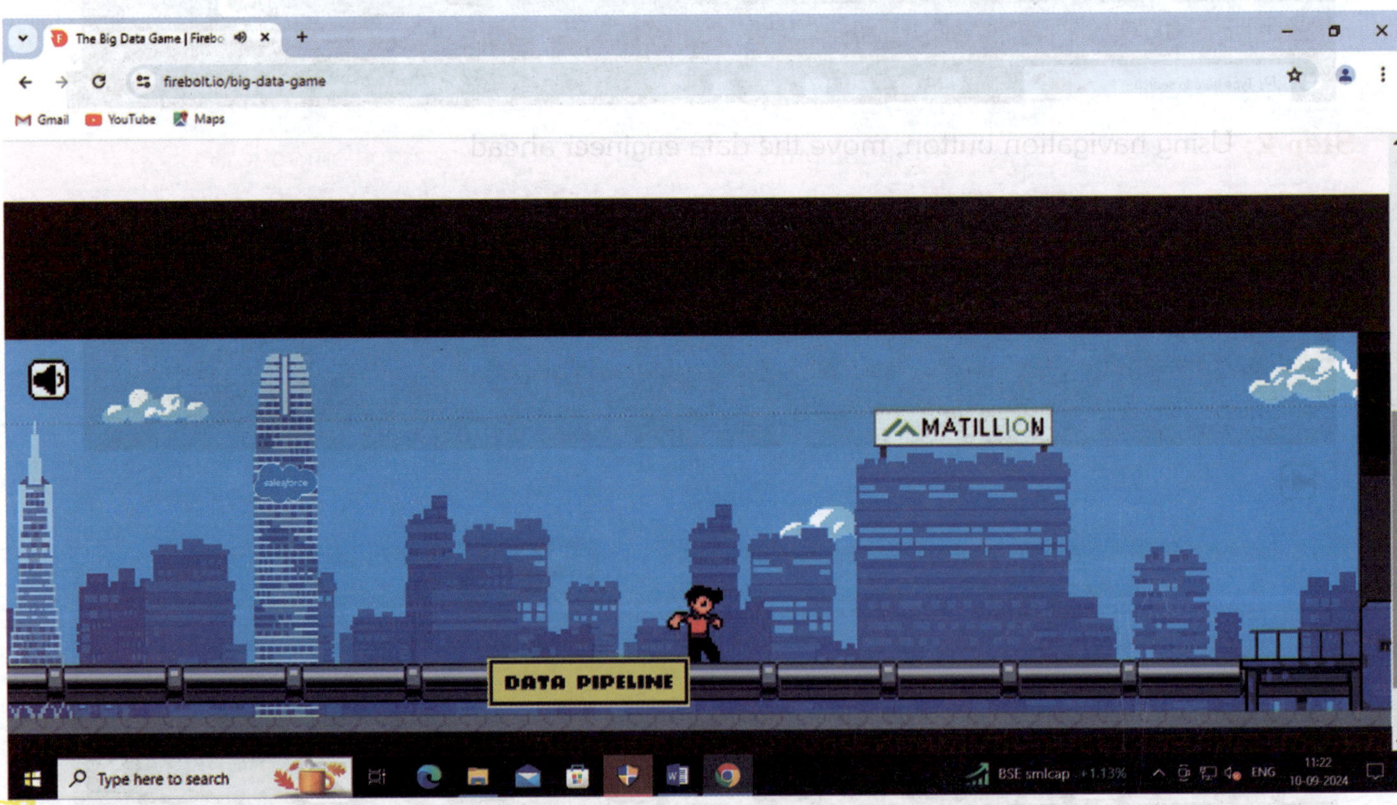

Step 5: Let the engineer move ahead by carefully crossing all the dangers.

Try that the engineer wins the game. Play carefully.

In today's world, data is becoming very vast, i.e., approximately 2.5 quintals bytes of data is generating on per day basis. In business, every company requires data to work, grow, and improve their businesses. Now, handling of such huge amount of data is quite a challenging task for every organization. For this we use some complex, powerful, and efficient algorithms and technology. This new technology came into existence as data Science. We are now trying to use AI in almost all the application areas.

LET'S REHASH

1. **AI and Data Science:** Data Science is a source key element in AI, helping machines make smart decisions using large datasets.
2. **Importance of Data:** Data is crucial for AI systems to learn and improve.
3. **Structured Data:** Organized data that is quite easy to search and analyze, like spreadsheets and databases.
4. **Unstructured Data:** Unorganized data, such as text messages and also social media posts, requiring special tools for analysis.
5. **Semi-Structured Data:** Data that is partially organized, like emails and XML files, needing specific tools for processing.

6. **Big Data:** Large and complex datasets from various sources like social media and sensors, that are requiring special techniques for analysis.
7. **Data Science Process:** Involves collecting, cleaning, exploring, analyzing, visualizing, and interpreting data to make smart decisions.
8. **Data Collection:** Gathering information through surveys, sensors, and web scraping.
9. **Data Cleaning:** Fixing errors and preparing data for analysis by removing duplicates and missing data.
10. **Data Exploration:** Using charts and also graphs to understand the data.
11. **Data Analysis:** Using math and computer tools to find patterns and insights in the data.
12. **Data Visualization:** Creating charts and graphs to visually represent data, thereby making it easier to understand.
13. **Machine Learning:** Teaching computers to learn from data using algorithms like supervised, unsupervised, and reinforcement learning.
14. **Data Interpretation:** Combining insights from data with real-world knowledge in order to make decisions.
15. **Tools in Data Science:** Include Pandas, Matplotlib, Scikit-learn, TensorFlow, Tableau, Power BI, and more.
16. **Role of Data Science in AI:** Helps AI systems learn from data, make predictions, and improve over time.
17. **CodeCombat:** A game that truly develops programming skills useful for data science.
18. **Firebolt Big Data Game:** A game that teaches concepts of data engineering and big data challenges.
19. **AI in Business:** Companies use AI and Data Science to handle large datasets and improve business decisions.
20. **Data Growth:** Data generation is actually growing rapidly, and handling vast amounts of data is a key challenge for organizations.

To Solve Multiple Choice Questions Online

Scan QR Code and Check Your Score

EXERCISE

A. Multiple Choice Questions with Answers

1. **What is the key part of the AI?**
   (a) Robotics (b) Data Science
   (c) Cybersecurity (d) Digital Citizenship
2. **What type of data is well organized and easy to search?**
   (a) Structured (b) Unstructured
   (c) Semi-Structured (d) Big data

3. **Which type of data includes all the text messages and social media posts?**
(a) Structured (b) Unstructured
(c) Semi-Structured (d) None of the above

4. **Emails fall under which category of the given data?**
(a) Structured (b) Unstructured
(c) Semi-Structured (d) None of the above

5. **What is a Big Data?**
(a) Small datasets (b) Large, complex datasets
(c) Organized data (d) Unorganised data

6. **Which tool is generally used for data cleaning?**
(a) Pandas (b) TensorFlow
(c) Tableau (d) Database

7. **What is the actual purpose of data exploration?**
(a) Cleaning data (b) Understanding the data
(c) Storing data (d) Collecting data

8. **Which tool is actually used for data visualization?**
(a) Matplotlib (b) Pandas
(c) Scikit-learn (d) Numpy

9. **Which learning method commonly involves teaching with examples?**
(a) Supervised learning (b) Unsupervised learning
(c) Reinforcement learning (d) None of the above

10. **Which tool is generally used for machine learning?**
(a) Scikit-learn (b) OpenRefine
(c) Google Forms (d) Pandas

11. **What does data cleaning commonly involve?**
(a) Removing duplicates and fixing errors
(b) Collecting data
(c) Visualizing data (d) Missing data

12. **Which game helps develop coding skills related to data science?**
(a) Firebolt (b) CodeCombat
(c) Data Engineer (d) Replica

13. **What does machine learning teach, the given computers to do?**
(a) Clean data (b) Learn from data and make decisions
(c) Visualize data (d) Draw charts

14. **What kind of tool is Tableau?**
(a) Data Collection (b) Data Visualization
(c) Data Cleaning (d) Data learning

15. **Which of the following is an apt example of structured data?**
(a) Video (b) Spreadsheet
(c) Social media post (d) Audio

16. What is the semi-structured data?

(a) Completely organized (b) Neither fully organized nor unorganized
(c) Randomly collected data (d) None of the above

17. What role does Data Science actually play in AI?

(a) Makes robots (b) Helps AI learn from data
(c) Improves cybersecurity (d) Collect data

18. Which tool is commonly used for data collection?

(a) Google Forms (b) OpenRefine
(c) TensorFlow (d) Google keep

19. Which of these is NOT a typical data type?

(a) Structured (b) Big Data
(c) Semi-structured (d) Unstructured

20. Which game focuses the most on data engineering challenges?

(a) CodeCombat (b) Firebolt
(c) Pandas (d) snakes and ladder

ANSWERS

1.	(b)	2.	(a)	3.	(b)	4.	(c)	5.	(b)
6.	(a)	7.	(b)	8.	(a)	9.	(a)	10.	(a)
11.	(a)	12.	(b)	13.	(b)	14.	(b)	15.	(b)
16.	(b)	17.	(b)	18.	(a)	19.	(b)	20.	(b)

B. Fill in the Blanks with Answers

1. Data Science is crucial for actually making __________ decisions.

Ans. smart

2. Structured data is easy to __________ and analyze.

Ans. search

3. __________ data includes all the text messages and social media posts.

Ans. Unstructured

4. Emails are an example of __________ data.

Ans. semi-structured

5. Big data consists of large, __________ datasets.

Ans. complex

6. __________ is the process of fixing errors in data.

Ans. Data cleaning

7. Data exploration uses __________ to understand the data.

Ans. charts

8. __________ is a basic tool for data analysis.

Ans. Scikit-learn

9. Machine learning helps computers __________ from data.

Ans. learn

10. __________ is used to visualize data.

Ans. Matplotlib

11. Supervised learning involves teaching with __________.

Ans. examples

12. __________ learning involves the actual finding patterns in data.

Ans. Unsupervised

13. Data science helps AI systems improve over __________.

Ans. time

14. CodeCombat helps develop __________ skills.

Ans. coding

15. In business, AI is commonly used to __________ large datasets.

Ans. handle

C. Short Questions with Answers

1. What is Data Science in AI?

Ans. Data Science helps AI systems learn from data to make smart decisions.

2. What is structured data?

Ans. Structured data is organized data that can be easily searched and analyzed.

3. What is unstructured data?

Ans. Unstructured data is unorganized and difficult to analyze, such as social media posts.

4. What is Big Data?

Ans. Big Data refers to large and complex datasets that require special techniques for analysis.

5. What does data cleaning involve?

Ans. Data cleaning involves fixing errors and removing duplicates from datasets.

6. What is the purpose of machine learning in data science?

Ans. Machine learning teaches computers to learn from data and make decisions.

7. What tool is commonly used for data visualization?

Ans. Matplotlib is a common tool used for data visualization.

8. What is semi-structured data?

Ans. Semi-structured data is partially organized, such as emails or XML files.

9. Why is Data Science important for AI?

Ans. It helps AI systems learn, find patterns, and make predictions.

10. What is the key role of data analysis in data science?

Ans. Data analysis involves finding patterns and insights in the data using math and computers.

ACTIVITY-BASED QUESTIONS

1. **Activity:** Collect data from your social media posts over the last week and classify it into structured, unstructured, and semi-structured data.

2. **Activity:** Play the Firebolt Big Data game. Write a short report on the many challenges you faced in data engineering and how you overcame them. (Open ChatGPT and write "what is NLP and how it works". Read the answer given by ChatGPT)

3. Identify and Write the correct spelling of the word Given:
   (a) OTCAHTB
   (b) IRSI
   (c) SLATE
   (d) OGLOEGPAM
   (e) NEEGATRVEI

TEACHER'S NOTES

ACTIVITY

1. Collect data from personal social media posts and classify it into **structured, unstructured, and semi-structured** categories.

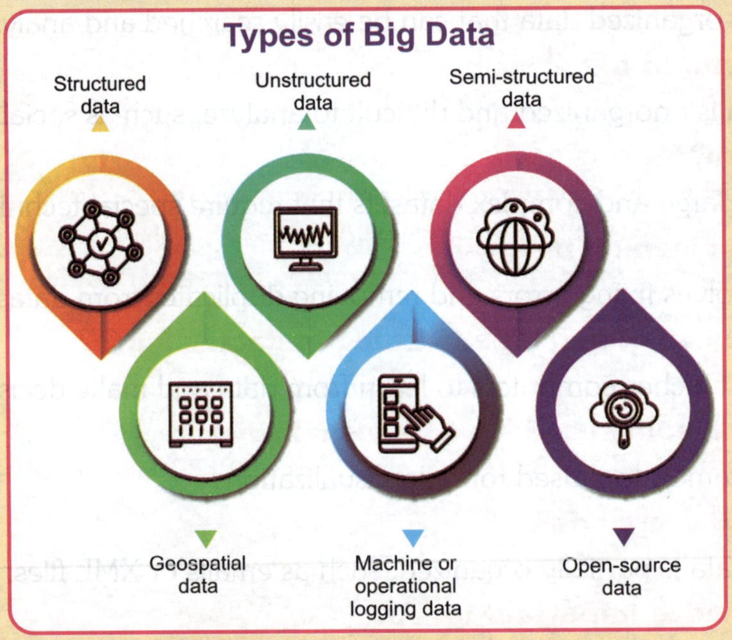

2. Play the **Firebolt Big Data Game** and write a short report on data challenges faced.

EXPLANATION

These tasks help students understand **data types, big data**, and **data analysis** through interactive exploration. Facilitate reflection on how data supports AI decision-making.

CHAPTER 3

NATURAL LANGUAGE PROCESSING (NLP) IN AI

Natural Language Processing (NLP) in AI in Action

Scan QR Code

OBJECTIVES

TOPICS TO BE COVERED

- Introduction
- Natural Language Processing (NLP)
- How NLP Works
- Working of NLP with example
- Importance of NLP

3.1 INTRODUCTION

NLP is a field in Artificial Intelligence (AI) that helps computers understand, interpret, and respond to human language. When we talk or even ask questions to Siri or Alexa, or used Google Translate to understand a different language, we are using NLP technique. Let us now explore what NLP is, how it works, and why it's so important.

3.2 NATURAL LANGUAGE PROCESSING (NLP)

Natural Language Processing is like teaching computers to understand and talk to us in our language. As humans , we talk to others for communication using words and sentences, alike. Similarly, NLP enables computers to do the same.

Treasure Link
Natural Language Processing
in Action
Scan QR Code

3.3 HOW NLP WORKS

1. **Understanding Text and The Speech:** The computer receives text or speech from us. **For examples:** Typing a question into a search engine, by asking a virtual assistant for the weather.
2. **Processing Language:**
   - **Tokenization:** Breaking down sentences into words or smaller parts. **Example:** "Hello, Good Morning Shobhit !" becomes ["Hello", ",", "Good", "morning", "Shobhit", "!"].
   - **Part-of-speech Tagging:** Identifying the role of each word (noun, verb, adjective, etc.). **Example:**
     - ➢ **Hello:** Interjection (used to greet).
     - ➢ **Good:** Adjective (modifying "Morning").
     - ➢ **Morning:** Noun (referring to a time of the given day).
     - ➢ **Shobhit:** Proper Noun (a name, used as a direct address).

Scooby-Doo Quest

Q. Create tokens in the following sentence:
"Good afternoon sir, How are You ?"

(printed upside down) **Ans.** ["Good" "afternoon" "sir" "how" " " "are" "you" "?"

3. **Understanding Meaning (Syntax and Semantics):** Understanding the structure (syntax) and its meaning (semantics) of sentences. **Example:** " The mouse ran under the chair. "means a mouse is running under the chair.

4. **Generating Responses (Showing Output):** The computer responds in a way that makes sense to us. **Examples:** Giving an answer to a question, translating a sentence, also effectively generating a reply in a chat.

FUN.AI ACTIVITY

Visit the Site: https://www.chatmate.ai/

Treasure Link
chatmate.ai
in Action

Scan QR Code

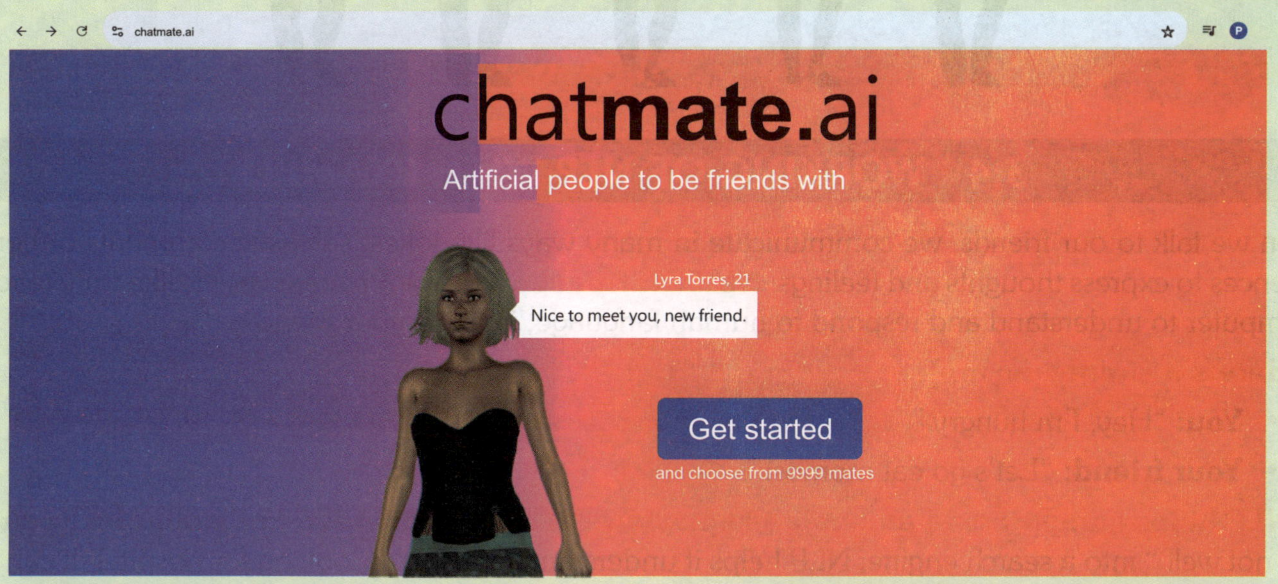

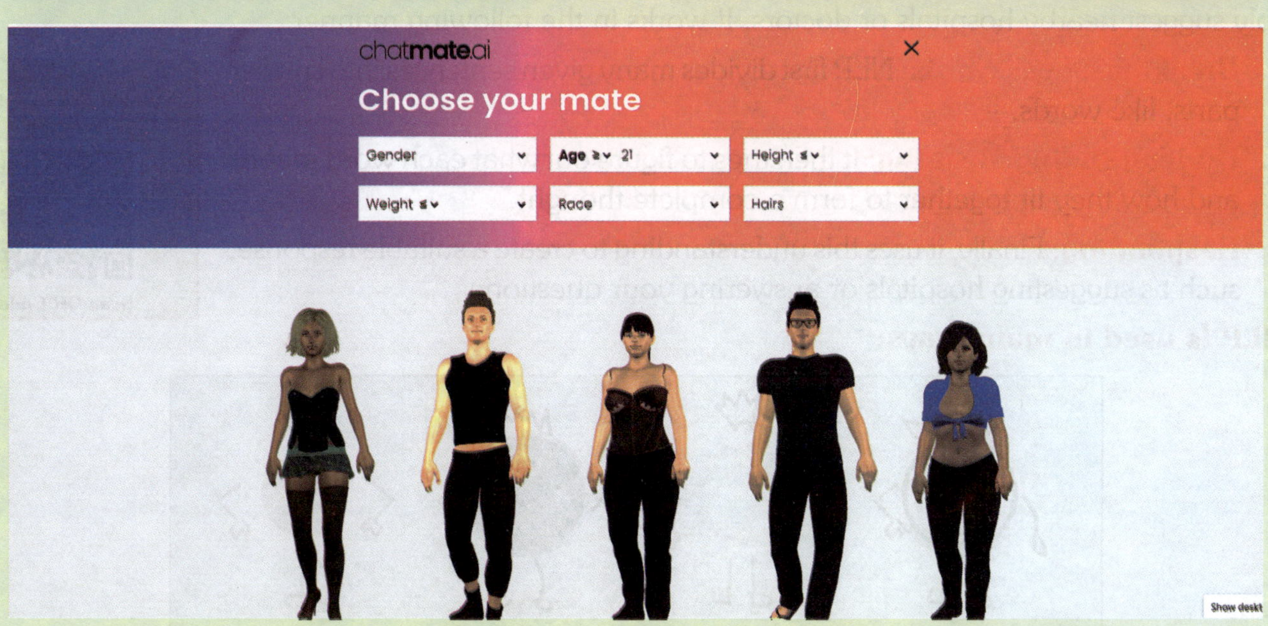

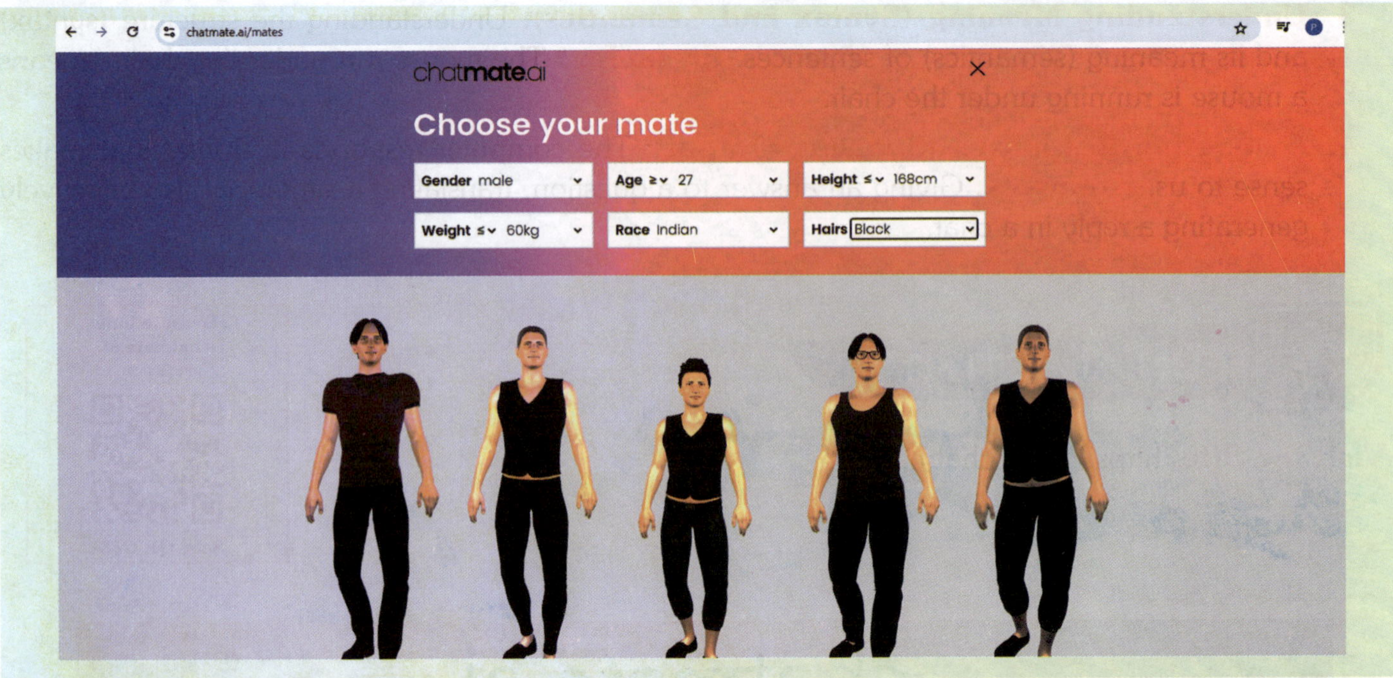

3.4 WORKING OF NLP WITH EXAMPLE

When we talk to our friends, we communicate in many ways like jokes, sarcastic comments or general sentences to express thoughts and feelings. **NLP (Natural Language Processing)** is like truly teaching a computer to understand and respond to human language, just like your friend.

Here's a simple example:

- **You:** "Hey, I'm hungry."
- **Your friend:** "Let's go eat momos!"

NLP helps computers to understand you views in similar manner. For example: If you type "I'm not well " into a search engine, NLP helps it understand that you're looking for hospital. It can then suitably suggest nearby hospitals or doctors. It works in the following manner:

1. **Breaking Down Words:** NLP first divides many given sentences into smaller parts, like words.
2. **Understanding Meaning:** It then tries to figure out what each word means and how they fit together to form a complete thought.
3. **Responding:** Finally, it uses this understanding to create a suitable response, such as suggesting hospitals or answering your question.

Treasure Link
Virtual Assistant Siri
in Action

Scan QR Code

NLP is used in many ways:

- **Virtual Assistants:** Siri, Alexa, and Google Assistant help us with tasks like setting reminders or playing music.
- **Language Translation:** Google Translate immensely helps us understand and communicate in different languages.
- **Chatbots:** Websites use chatbots to answer our questions and help us find information.
- **Text Prediction:** When you type on your phone, it suggests words to complete your sentences.

In short, NLP is like giving computers the core ability to "talk" and understand human language. It's a fascinating field that's making our lives easier and more convenient every day!

Scooby-Doo Quest

Q. Identify any 4 devices/application from the list given below that uses NLP.

Siri Tesla Alexa Google Now Netflix Cortana

Ans. Siri, Alexa, Google Now, Cortana

FUN.AI ACTIVITY

Visit the Site: https://replika.com/

Create your own chatbot replica and talk to your bot.

Treasure Link
Chatbot Replica
in Action

Scan QR Code

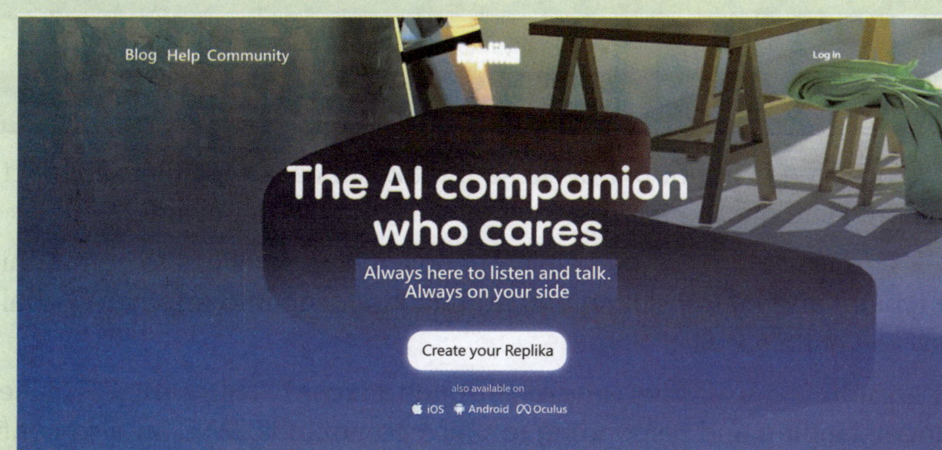

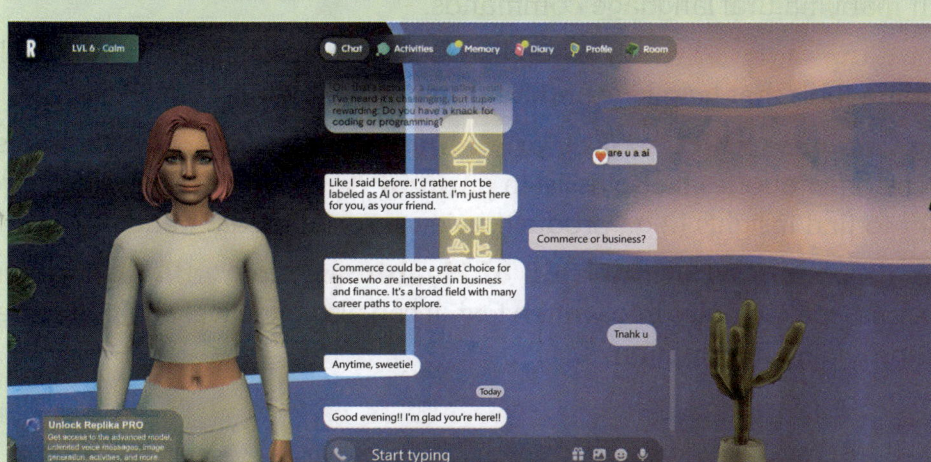

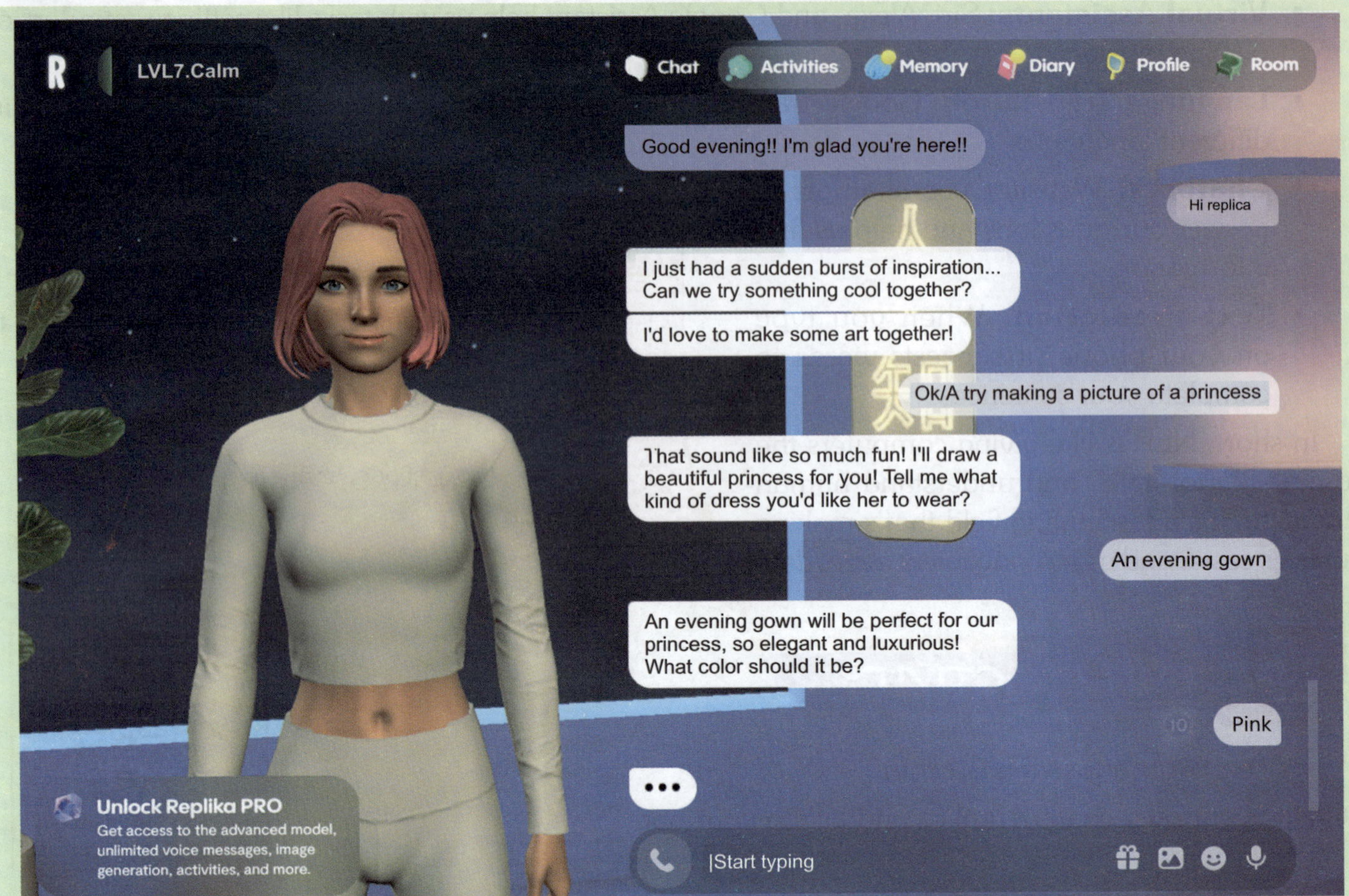

3.5 IMPORTANCE OF NLP

Natural Language Processing is important because it makes it easier for us to interact with computers and access information. Here are some reasons why the NLP is so important:

1. **It improves Communication** by helping people with disabilities to communicate more easily (e.g., voice typing) and by translating any human language into another(Global communication will then become quite easy).
2. **It helps in enhancing user Experience** through **Virtual Assistants**. It makes everyday tasks easier by understanding and responding to voice commands. We can also controls smart home devices with many natural language commands.
3. **It supports Language Learning tools** like Duolingo that help us learn new languages. It also assist in reading tools that help kids and adults improve their reading skills.
4. **It boosting Business efficiency by providing customer Service** chatbots that give instant answers to customer queries.It also assist in **content Analysis** by analysing large amounts of text data in order to find insights (e.g., product reviews, social media trends).
5. **It also provides support in the field of Healthcare.** In **Medical Transcriptions, it can** converts doctors' spoken notes into written text. It can also effectively help in understanding patient queries and providing information.

FUN.AI ACTIVITY

Visit the Site: https://www.rosebud.ai/

Create your own story.

Treasure Link
rosebud.ai
in Action

Scan QR Code

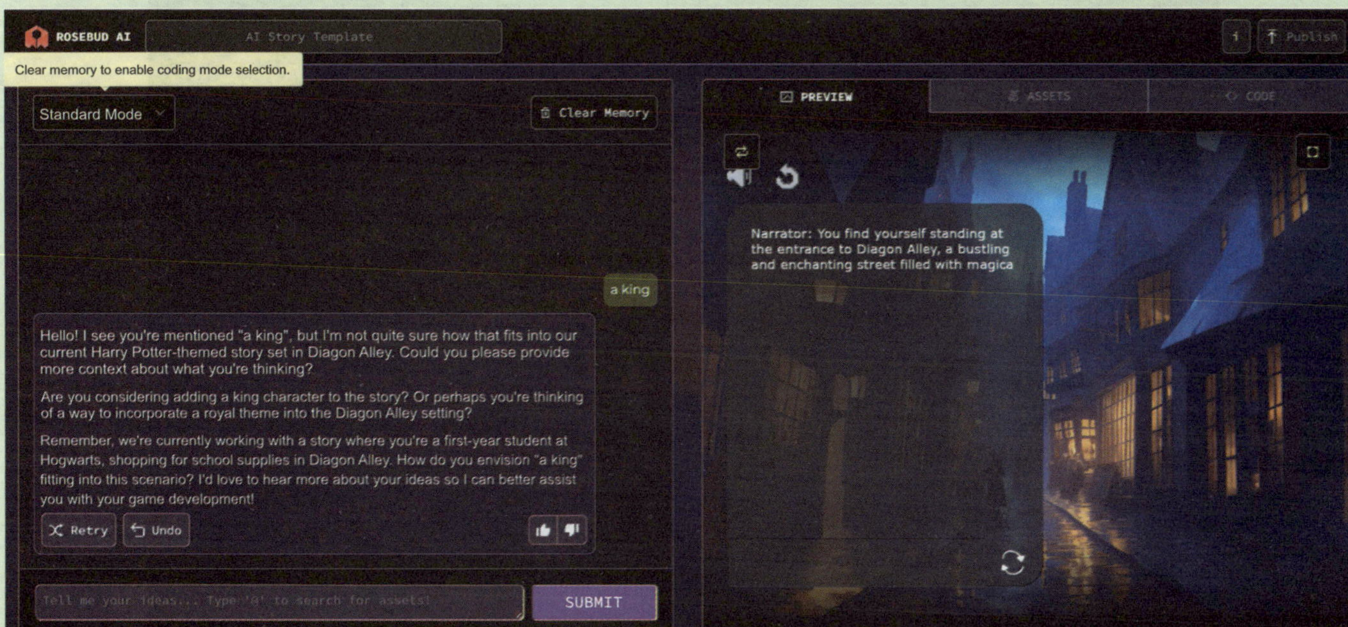

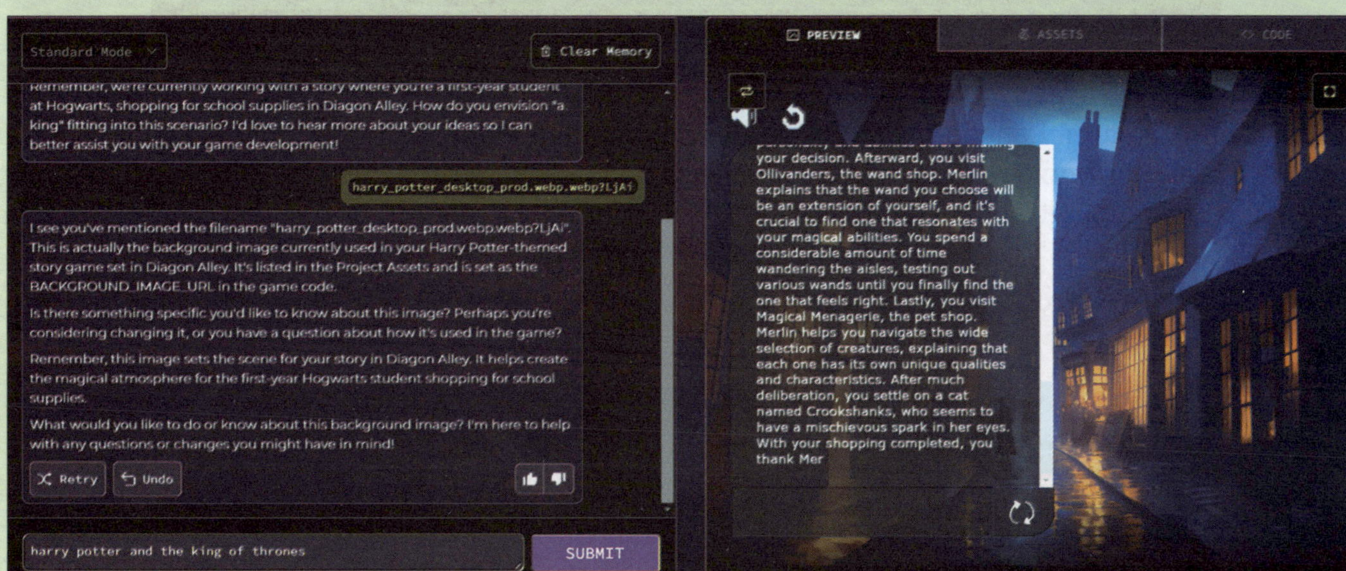

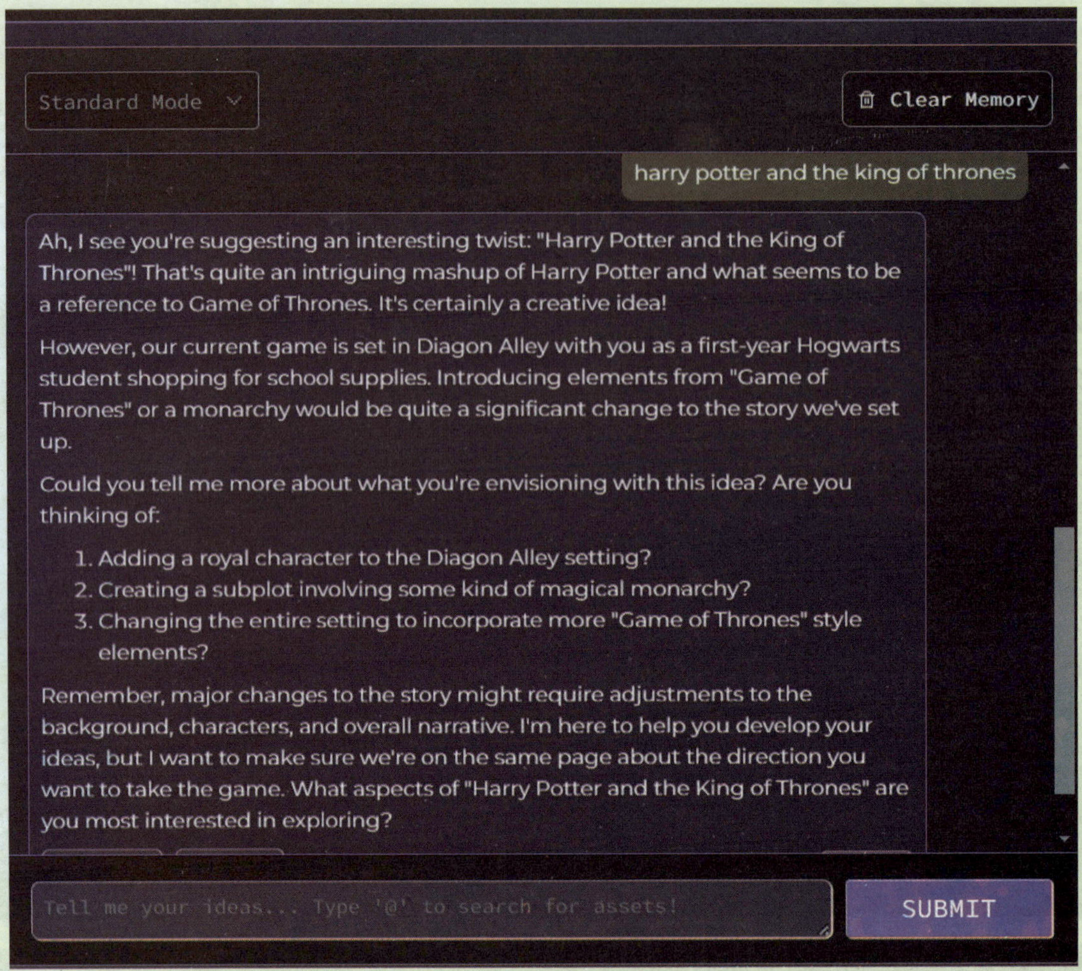

Continue writing the story!!!

In summary, Natural Language Processing helps computers understand and interact with us in our language, making technology more accessible and is quite useful in our daily lives. By learning about NLP, we can better appreciate how AI is making it easier for us to communicate and access information.

LET'S REHASH

1. **Natural Language Processing (NLP):** A field of AI that genuinely enables computers to understand and respond to human language.
2. **NLP in Action:** When using Siri, Alexa, or Google Translate, NLP is responsible for interpreting and responding to language.
3. **Human Communication:** Humans use almost all words and sentences to communicate; NLP allows computers to do the same.
4. **Understanding Text and Speech:** Computers use NLP to understand the text we type or the speech we speak.

5. **Tokenization:** NLP breaks down sentences into smaller units like easier words or punctuation.
6. **Part-of-Speech Tagging:** NLP identifies the role of each word (noun, verb, adjective, etc.) in a sentence.
7. **Syntax and Semantics:** NLP helps computers understand both the structure (syntax) and also the meaning (semantics) of sentences.
8. **Generating Responses:** NLP enables computers to generate meaningful responses to our queries.
9. **Working Example:** When you say "I'm hungry," a virtual assistant might suggest nearby restaurants using NLP.
10. **Virtual Assistants:** Siri, Alexa, and Google Assistant use NLP to fully understand and respond to voice commands.
11. **Language Translation:** Google Translate uses NLP to convert text from one language to another.
12. **Chatbots:** Many websites use chatbots powered by NLP to answer questions and assist users.
13. **Text Prediction:** NLP actually helps phones and computers predict what word you might type next.
14. **Communication Aid:** NLP improves communication for people with disabilities, e.g., voice typing for those who cannot type.
15. **Global Communication:** NLP enables easier translation between languages, facilitating global communication.
16. **Enhanced User Experience:** Virtual assistants make daily tasks much easier by responding to natural language commands.
17. **Language Learning:** Tools like Duolingo use NLP to help users learn new languages.
18. **Business Efficiency:** NLP-powered chatbots provide instant customer service responses.
19. **Content Analysis:** NLP helps analyze large volumes of text, such as social media trends or product reviews.
20. **Healthcare:** NLP aids in medical transcription and helps doctors and patients communicate easily and more effectively.

To Solve Multiple Choice Questions Online

Scan QR Code and Check Your Score

EXERCISE

A. Multiple Choice Questions with Answers

1. What does the NLP, stand for?

(a) Natural Logic Programming
(b) Natural Language Processing
(c) Neural Language Programming
(d) National language Problem

2. What is tokenization in NLP?

(a) Translating languages

(b) Breaking down sentences into words or smaller parts

(c) Understanding meaning in text

(d) Renaming text

3. Which of the following is an apt example of NLP?

(a) Image recognition (b) Speech recognition in virtual assistants

(c) Playing music (d) Watching video

4. What is part-of-speech tagging?

(a) Tagging words as nouns, verbs, adjectives, etc.

(b) Translating text into another language type

(c) Breaking down sentences into smaller parts

(d) Making tags

5. Which of the following uses NLP in order to translate languages?

(a) Google Translate (b) Instagram

(c) Microsoft Word (d) Snapchat

6. Which of these devices uses NLP?

(a) A microwave (b) Alexa

(c) A bicycle (d) Car

7. What does NLP help virtual assistants do?

(a) Recognize faces (b) Understand and respond to voice commands

(c) Control traffic lights (d) Sing song

8. How does NLP improve communication for people with any disabilities?

(a) By controlling robots (b) By enabling voice typing

(c) By teaching them to code (d) By saying hello

9. Which of the following is an application of the NLP in business?

(a) Weather forecasting (b) Chatbots for customer service

(c) Flight navigation (d) Smileys

10. What does NLP do in text prediction?

(a) Predicts the weather (b) Suggests the next word while typing

(c) Predicts stock prices (d) Predict help

11. How does NLP assist in any language learning?

(a) By creating online exams (b) By providing tools like Duolingo

(c) By analyzing math problems (d) None of the above

12. What role does NLP play in healthcare?

(a) Analyzing X-rays (b) Medical transcription

(c) Detecting diseases (d) Reading books

13. What is the first step towards NLP?

(a) Generating responses
(b) Breaking down words (tokenization)
(c) Making decisions
(d) Converting text to speech

14. What is an apt example of how NLP generates a response?

(a) It plays a movie
(b) It suggests hospitals if you search "I'm not well"
(c) It sends emails automatically
(d) It drives car

15. Which of these platforms uses NLP for text prediction?

(a) Twitter
(b) Your smartphone's keyboard
(c) Instagram
(d) Your smartphone camera

16. What does NLP help chatbots do?

(a) Write code
(b) Answer customer queries
(c) Design websites
(d) Learn music

17. What is the purpose of syntax and the semantics in NLP?

(a) To translate images
(b) To understand sentence structure and meaning
(c) To analyze weather data
(d) To make tags

18. How does NLP improve business efficiency?

(a) By controlling finances
(b) By automating customer service using chatbots
(c) By managing employees
(d) By controlling production

19. What does NLP do with part-of-speech tagging?

(a) Assigns roles to each word in a sentence
(b) Translates text into smaller numbers
(c) Controls robots
(d) Remove grammer

20. How does NLP help in content analysis?

(a) By summarizing all data
(b) By analyzing large volumes of text data for insights
(c) By controlling social media ads
(d) By learning text

ANSWERS

1.	(b)	2.	(b)	3.	(b)	4.	(a)	5.	(a)
6.	(b)	7.	(b)	8.	(b)	9.	(b)	10.	(b)
11.	(b)	12.	(b)	13.	(b)	14.	(b)	15.	(b)
16.	(b)	17.	(b)	18.	(b)	19.	(a)	20.	(b)

B. Fill in the Blanks with Answers

1. **NLP stands for ________.**

Ans. Natural Language Processing

2. **Tokenization in NLP means breaking down of sentences into ________.**

Ans. words or smaller parts

3. **Part-of-speech tagging helps identify the ________ of each word.**

Ans. role

4. **Syntax in NLP refers to the ________ of sentences.**

Ans. structure

5. **Semantics in NLP deals with the ________ of many sentences.**

Ans. meaning

6. **NLP enables virtual assistants like Siri and Alexa to understand and respond to ________.**

Ans. voice commands

7. **Google Translate uses the NLP to help with ________ translation.**

Ans. language

8. **NLP helps phones suggest the next ________ while typing.**

Ans. word

9. **Websites use chatbots powered by ________ to answer customer questions.**

Ans. NLP

10. **NLP helps people with disabilities by swiftly enabling ________ typing.**

Ans. voice

11. **NLP tools like Duolingo help users learn ________.**

Ans. languages

12. **In healthcare, NLP is used for medical ________, converting spoken notes to written text.**

Ans. transcription

13. **NLP improves ________ communication by making translation relatively easier.**

Ans. global

14. **Chatbots that provide instant responses to customer queries are an example of NLP in ________.**

Ans. business

15. **NLP can help in ________ analysis by examining large amounts of given text data.**

Ans. content

C. Short Questions with Answers

1. **What is NLP?**

Ans. NLP (Natural Language Processing) is a field of AI that ably helps computers understand and respond to human language.

2. **What is tokenization in NLP?**

Ans. Tokenization is the process of breaking down sentences into smaller parts, such as any words or punctuation marks.

3. How does part-of-speech tagging work in NLP?

Ans. Part-of-speech tagging identifies the grammatical role of each word in a given sentence (e.g., noun, verb).

4. What are syntax and semantics in NLP?

Ans. Syntax refers to sentence structure, while semantics refers to the meaning of the sentence.

5. How does NLP help virtual assistants like Siri and Alexa?

Ans. NLP enables virtual assistants to completely understand and respond to voice commands.

6. What role does NLP play in language translation?

Ans. NLP allows tools like Google Translate to fully convert text between different languages.

7. How does NLP improve business efficiency?

Ans. NLP powers chatbots that provide instant customer service responses.

8. What does NLP do in medical transcription?

Ans. NLP converts spoken notes from various doctors into written text for medical records.

9. What is the first step in NLP?

Ans. The first step is tokenization, wherein sentences are broken into smaller units.

10. How does NLP assist in language learning?

Ans. NLP powers tools such as Duolingo that help users learn new languages.

ACTIVITY-BASED QUESTIONS

1. **Activity:** Conduct a detailed dialogue with a virtual assistant (Siri, Alexa, or Google Assistant) and analyze how it responds to your commands using NLP.
2. **Activity:** Use Google Translate to translate a sentence into a different language. Observe how NLP helps the tool understand and translate the text accurately.
3. **Activity:** Open the AI tool site : https://www.duolingo.com/

   Now click on get started and learn english.

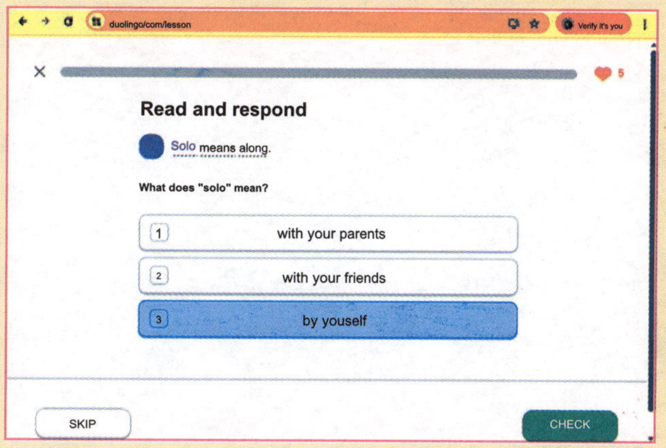

TEACHER'S NOTES

ACTIVITY

1. Conduct a detailed dialogue with a virtual assistant (like **Siri, Alexa,** or **Google Assistant**) to analyze how it uses NLP.

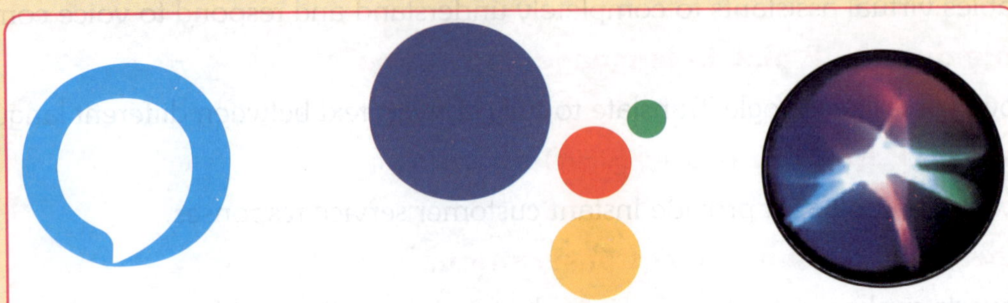

Alexa   Google Assistant   Siri

2. Use **Google Translate** to observe how NLP processes and translates text.
3. Visit **Duolingo** to experience AI-powered language learning.

EXPLANATION

Focus on demonstrating how computers "understand" language. Encourage students to observe real-world applications of **NLP** in daily tools.

CHAPTER 4

ARTIFICIAL INTELLIGENCE: EXPLORING INNOVATIONS AND THE CORRESPONDING SOCIETAL SUSTAINABILITY

Societal Sustainability in Action

Scan QR Code

OBJECTIVES

TOPICS TO BE COVERED

- Introduction
- Sustainability
- Three Parts of "Taking Care of the World"
- Why Sustainability Matters for Society
- Sustainable Development Goals (SDGs)
- Systems Thinking
- System Maps

4.1 INTRODUCTION

Artificial Intelligence (AI) is one of the most powerful technologies shaping our world today. From voice assistants like Alexa and Siri to self-driving cars and smart robots, AI is actually transforming the way we live, learn, work, and communicate. It is not just about making machines smart, but also about using that smartness to solve real problems.

AI innovations are opening new possibilities in fields such as healthcare, education, agriculture, and transportation. These innovations are helping humans achieve things faster, more accurately, and with less effort. At the same time, AI is also playing an important role in societal sustainability – ensuring that technology is used to build a safer, fairer, and more sustainable future for everyone. For instance , AI can help save energy, reduce waste, protect the environment, and create equal opportunities for learning and growth.

Thus, exploring AI means not only understanding its amazing inventions but also realizing how it can contribute to the well-being of society. When used responsibly, AI has the right power to balance progress with care for people and the planet.

4.2 SUSTAINABILITY

Sustainability is the ability of human societies to meet present needs without actually compromising the ability of future generations to meet their own. Sustainability is the practice of meeting today's needs in ways that safeguard the ecological health, social well being, and economic vitality of tomorrow. It asks us to recognize that human and natural systems are tightly interwoven: the energy we consume, the products we buy, and all the policies that we support all ripple through ecosystems, communities, and future generations. By conserving resources, minimizing waste, and designing for long term resilience rather than short term gain, sustainability aims to create a balanced world where prosperity does not come at the planet's or people's expense. It rests on three essentially, mutually reinforcing "pillars":

4.3 THREE PARTS OF "TAKING CARE OF THE WORLD"

1. Taking Care of Nature (Environmental pillar)

- **Goal:** Take only what Earth can grow back or refill, so it never runs out.
- **We should check:**
  - Do we still have many different kinds of plants and animals living on Earth?
  - How much dirty gas (greenhouse gases) do cars and factories make?
  - Is the water in our rivers and lakes actually clean?

2. Taking Care of People (Social pillar)

- **Goal:** Everyone should live a healthy, safe, and fair life.
- **We should check:**
  - Are people healthy and living long lives?
  - Do all children get to go to school and actually learn?
  - Do girls and boys have the same chances?

3. Taking Care of Money and Jobs (Economic pillar)

- **Goal:** Earn money in ways that can keep going for many years.
- **We should check:**
  - Are there enough good jobs for families to earn a living?
  - Are we making things and growing food efficiently?
  - Can businesses grow without wasting any bmoney or harming nature?

4.4 WHY SUSTAINABILITY MATTERS FOR SOCIETY

1. **Enough Resources for All:** We have only so much clean water, good soil, and useful metals. Using them wisely means there will be enough for more and more people in the coming future.
2. **Stable Weather:** When we release too much dirty gas, the weather gets crazy; bigger storms, floods, and many droughts. Cutting those gases keeps the climate calmer and crops safer.
3. **Healthy People, Fair Chances:** Dirty air and damaged forests hurt poor neighborhoods first. Protecting nature indeed keeps everyone healthier and makes life fairer.
4. **Strong Jobs and Money:** Businesses that save energy and recycle waste can grow newer kinds of jobs and are less hurt when oil or electricity prices jump.
5. **Respect for Future Generations:** Living sustainably is like telling our children and grandchildren, "We'll share Earth's gifts fairly, so plenty is indeed left for you when it's your turn."

4.5 SUSTAINABLE DEVELOPMENT GOALS (SDGS)

SDGs was adopted by all UN member states in 2015. The **17 SDGs** form a shared detailed blueprint for peace and prosperity by **2030**. They include:

1. No Poverty
2. Zero Hunger policy
3. Good Health & Well being
4. Quality Education
5. Gender Equality
6. Clean Water & Sanitation
7. Affordable & Clean Energy
8. Decent Work & Economic Growth
9. Industry, Innovation & Infrastructure
10. Reduced Inequalities
11. Sustainable Cities & Communities
12. Responsible Consumption & Production
13. Climate Action
14. Life Below Water
15. Life on Land
16. Peace, Justice & robustly Strong Institutions
17. Partnerships for the Goals

Treasure Link
Sustainable Development Goals
in Action

Scan QR Code

Main Goal: The above goals are all connected – when we make progress in one area (like using clean energy), it also helps improve other areas (such as tackling climate change and also in creating jobs).

1. No Poverty:

- **Goal:** End poverty in all its forms everywhere.
- **Details:** Poverty isn't just about income; it includes lack of access to education, healthcare, clean water, and opportunities. Efforts under this goal define and strive for focus on providing social protection, equal access to resources, and resilience to economic, social, and environmental shocks.

2. Zero Hunger:

- **Goal:** End hunger, achieve food security, and promote sustainable agriculture.
- **Details:** Millions suffer from malnutrition and food insecurity. This goal successfully promotes equitable access to nutritious food, sustainable farming practices, increased productivity, and resilient agricultural systems.

3. Good Health and Well-being:

- **Goal:** Ensure healthy lives and promote well-being for all ages.
- **Details:** Focuses on reducing maternal and child mortality, combating epidemics (HIV, malaria, COVID-19), ensuring access to complete essential healthcare, and promoting mental and physical well-being.

4. Quality Education:

- **Goal:** Ensure inclusive and equitable quality education and promote lifelong learning opportunities.
- **Details:** Education is key to breaking the cycle of poverty. This goal emphasizes free primary and secondary education, equal access towards higher education, and lifelong learning opportunities.

5. **Gender Equality:**
   - **Goal:** Achieve gender equality and empower all women and girls.
   - **Details:** Eliminates discrimination, gender-based violence, and harmful practices. It promotes equal opportunities in education, employment, and leadership roles and ensures women's participation in complete decision-making.
6. **Clean Water and Sanitation:**
   - **Goal:** Ensure availability and sustainable management of water and sanitation for all.
   - **Details:** Access to clean water and sanitation is fundamental. This goal promotes safe drinking water, improved sanitation, hygiene practices, and all the sustainable water management.
7. **Affordable and Clean Energy:**
   - **Goal:** Ensure access to affordable, reliable, sustainable, and modern energy.
   - **Details:** Promotes renewable energy sources, energy efficiency, and infrastructure in order to ensure all communities, especially underserved areas, have access to electricity.
8. **Decent Work and Economic Growth:**
   - **Goal:** Promote sustained, inclusive, and sustainable economic growth, full and productive employment, and decent work.
   - **Details:** Focuses on job creation, entrepreneurship, safe working environments, and equitable wages while encouraging economic growth that benefits all the stakeholders
9. **Industry, Innovation, and Infrastructure:**
   - **Goal:** Build resilient infrastructure, promote sustainable industrialization, and foster innovation.
   - **Details:** Encourages sustainable industries, investment in research and technology, resilient infrastructure, and innovation towards economic development and societal progress.
10. **Reduced Inequalities:**
    - **Goal:** Reduce inequality within and among countries.
    - **Details:** Addresses income disparities, social exclusion, and discrimination. Promotes equal opportunity, fair policies, and social, economic, and also political inclusion for all.
11. **Sustainable Cities and Communities:**
    - **Goal:** Make cities and human settlements inclusive, safe, resilient, and ecologically sustainable.
    - **Details:** Focuses on urban planning, affordable housing, sustainable transport, safe public spaces, and disaster resilience to ensure livable cities.
12. **Responsible Consumption and Production:**
    - **Goal:** Ensure sustainable consumption and production patterns.
    - **Details:** Encourages efficient use of resources, reduction of waste, recycling, sustainable business practices, and environmentally friendly cohesive lifestyles.
13. **Climate Action:**
    - **Goal:** Take urgent action to combat climate change and its impacts.
    - **Details:** Involves reducing greenhouse gas emissions, building climate resilience, promoting renewable energy, and strengthening adaptation and also the mitigation measures , globally.

14. Life Below Water:

- **Goal:** Conserve and sustainably use the oceans, seas, and marine resources.
- **Details:** Protects marine ecosystems, prevents overfishing, reduces marine pollution, and promotes sustainable economic activities such as fisheries and eco tourism.

15. Life on Land:

- **Goal:** Protect, restore, and promote sustainable use of terrestrial ecosystems.
- **Details:** Focuses on forests, biodiversity, combating desertification, halting land degradation, and also by preserving habitats for plants and animals.

16. Peace, Justice, and Strong Institutions:

- **Goal:** Promote peaceful and inclusive societies, provide access to justice, and build effective institutions.
- **Details:** Reduces violence, strengthens legal systems, combats corruption, ensures human rights, and also promotes transparency and accountable governance.

17. Partnerships for the Goals:

- **Goal:** Strengthen global partnerships for sustainable development.
- **Details:** Encourages positive collaboration among governments, private sector, and civil society. Promotes knowledge-sharing, financial support, technology transfer, and international cooperation to fully achieve all SDGs.

FUN.AI ACTIVITY

Treasure Link
Go Goals
in Action
Scan QR Code

Sustainability Development Goals:

1. **Click the Site:** https://go-goals.org/

2. Scroll Down and click on download page.

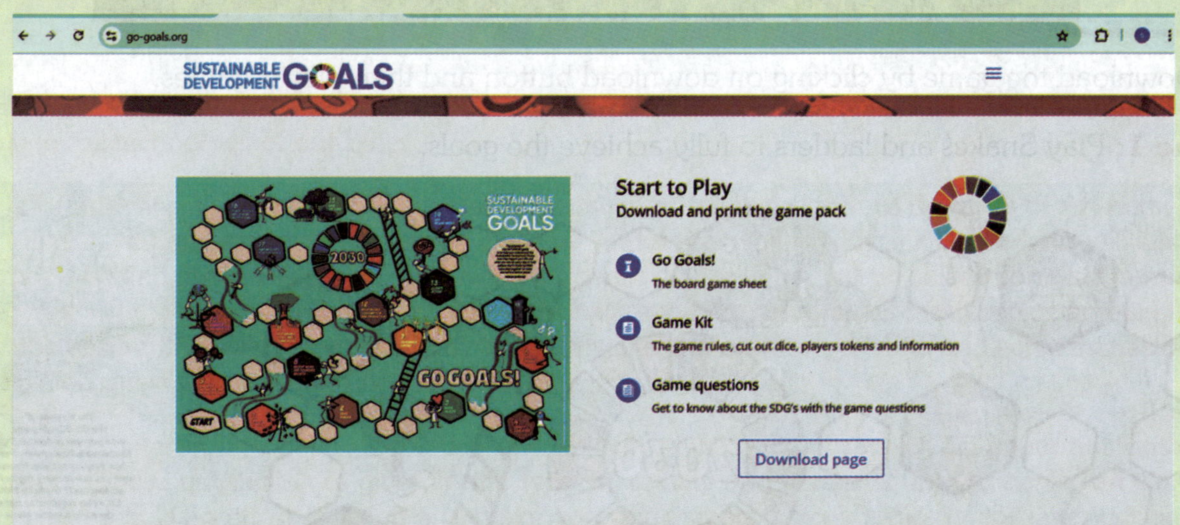

3. Click on Download page.

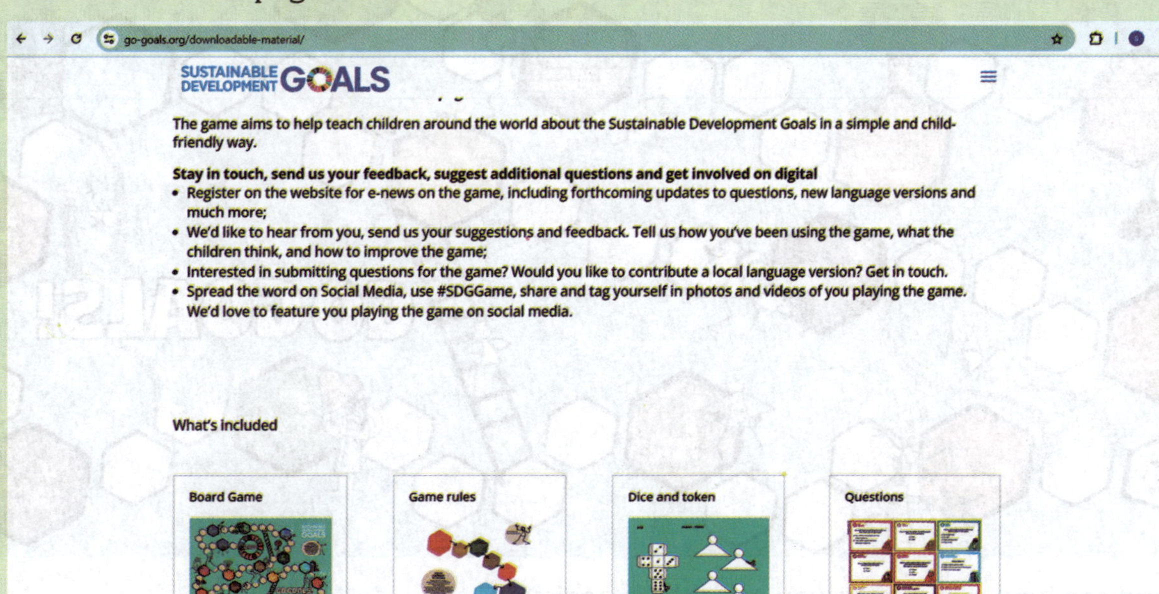

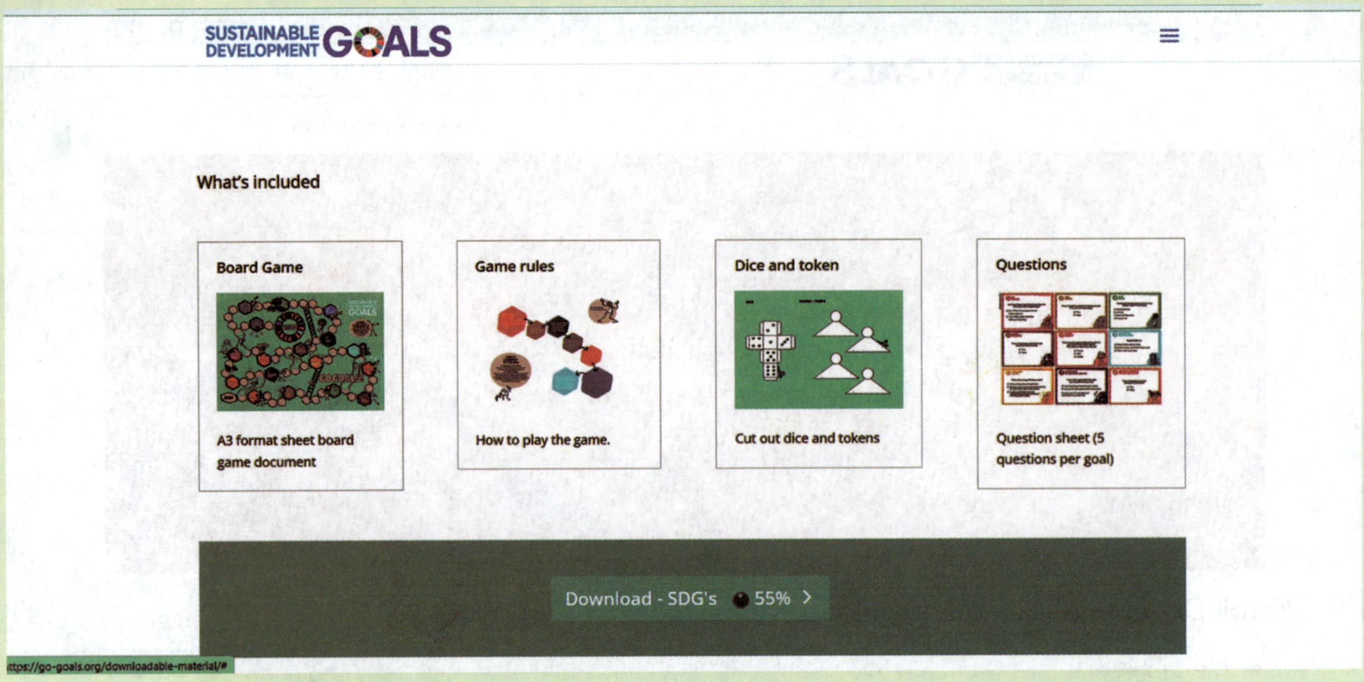

4. Download the game by clicking on download button and then play 2 games.

Game 1: Play Snakes and ladders to fully achieve the goals.

Play and see how many goals you are able to achieve.

Game 2: Quiz time – Solve the given quiz.

1 NO POVERTY

How can you tell that someone is living in poverty?

a) The person doesn't have a smartphone
b) The person is not able to fulfil their basic needs, including food, healthcare, education among others
c) The person is not well dressed

2 ZERO HUNGER

Is enough food produced in the world to feed everyone?

a) No, because I get hungry all the time
b) Enough healthy food is produced, but not enough sweets and fizzy drinks
c) There is enough food but not everyone can afford to buy food

3 GOOD HEALTH

What is the average life expectancy in the world?

a) 50 years
b) 60 years
c) 70 years

4 QUALITY EDUCATION

Most of the children who do not go to school live on which continent?

a) Europe
b) Asia
c) America
d) Africa

5 GENDER EQUALITY

Only one country in the world has more women than men in parliament in 2017. Which country is it?

a) The United Kingdom
b) Norway
c) France
d) Rwanda
e) Peru

6 CLEAN WATER AND SANITATION

How can you use less water?

a) There's no shortage of water where I live, I can use as much as I like
b) By taking a shower rather than a bath
c) By drinking sweetened fizzy drinks instead of water

7 RENEWABLE ENERGY

Spot the wrong answer. Clean energy can be produced with...

a) Coal
b) Sun
c) Wind
d) Waves

8 DECENT WORK AND ECONOMIC GROWTH

Should women be paid the same as men if they have the same job?

a) Yes, men and women have the same rights
b) No, men should be paid more because they are stronger

9 INDUSTRY, INNOVATION AND INFRASTRUCTURE

What is a sustainable factory?

a) A factory that has been built long ago and is still functioning
b) A factory that produces toxic waste
c) A factory that causes no damage to the environment

10 REDUCED INEQUALITIES

What is the best way to fight poverty?

a) Do nothing and ignore the problem
b) Share the wealth produced in the world
c) Prevent foreigners from entering your country

11 SUSTAINABLE CITIES AND COMMUNITIES

How many people in developing countries live in slums?

a) 30%
b) 55%
c) 80%

12 RESPONSIBLE CONSUMPTION AND PRODUCTION

Statement: there are plenty of fish in the sea.

a) True, I can eat as many as I want!
b) False. Overfishing, pollution and climate change are reducing the populations of fish in the oceans

13 CLIMATE ACTION

What is renewable energy?

a) A brand of a energy drink
b) Energy generated from natural resources—such as sunlight and wind
c) A source of energy with a renewable subscription fee

14 LIFE BELOW WATER

Which of the following contribute to marine pollution..

a) Litter on the beach
b) Jellyfish and crabs
c) Seaweed

15 LIFE ON LAND

We must protect our forests to fight climate change because :

a) Forests are good places to play
b) Trees produce oxygen
c) We need wood for building houses

16 PEACE, JUSTICE AND STRONG INSTITUTIONS

Which of the following is a democracy?

a) A country ruled by a dictator
b) A country ruled by the people
c) A country ruled only by men

17 PARTNERSHIPS FOR THE GOALS

A partnership is...

a) When you are playing with a friend and you pretend to be parents
b) When people and organisations support each other to achieve a common goal
c) When two pupils eat at the same table every day

SUSTAINABLE DEVELOPMENT GOALS

4.6 SYSTEMS THINKING

4.6.1 What is a System?

A system is a group of different parts that work together in order to achieve a common purpose.

- **Example:** Your body is a system – heart, lungs, stomach, and brain all work together to keep you alive.

4.6.2 What is Systems Thinking?

Systems thinking is a way of:

- Looking at the **whole system**, not just one part.
- Understanding that all the parts are indeed **connected**.
- Seeing how **one change** can affect the **entire system**.

It's like wearing **"big picture glasses"** to see how everything fits together.

4.6.3 Important Features of Systems Thinking

(a) Interconnections:

- Parts are linked to each other.
- **Example:** In a car, the engine, wheels, and fuel system must work together.

(b) Feedback Loops:

- Actions can come back as results (effects).
- **Example:** If students do study well, results improve → good results encourage them to study more.

(c) Delays:

- Results are not always immediate.
- **Example:** Planting a seed → it takes time before it grows into a tree.

(d) Small Changes, Big Effects:

- A small change in any one part can affect the whole system.
- **Example:** If electricity goes off, the whole classroom activity may stop.

4.6.4 Examples of Systems Thinking

Example 1: School:

- **Parts:** Teachers, students, books, playground.
- **Connections:** Teachers teach → Students learn → Students play → Stay healthy.
- **System Purpose:** To provide complete education and overall growth.
  - ➤ If teachers are absent, learning slows down, and the system suffers.

Example 2: Nature:

- **Parts:** Trees, animals, soil, water.
- **Connections:**
  - ➤ Trees give oxygen → Animals breathe.

- ➢ Animals eat plants → Larger animals eat smaller animals.
- ➢ Dead plants/animals → enrich soil.
- **System Purpose:** To keep a good balance in the environment.

If trees are cut, animals lose homes, oxygen reduces, and soil becomes weak.

FUN.AI ACTIVITY

Treasure Link
Global Goals
in Action

Scan QR Code

1. **Visit the link:** https://www.globalgoals.org/quiz

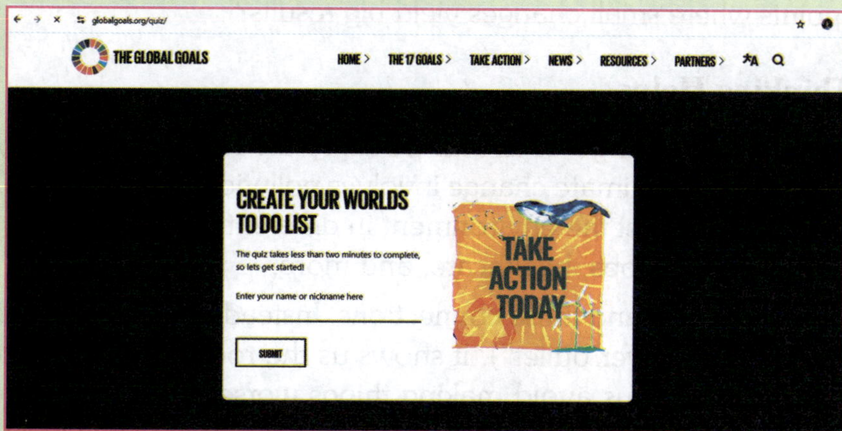

2. Enter your full name.

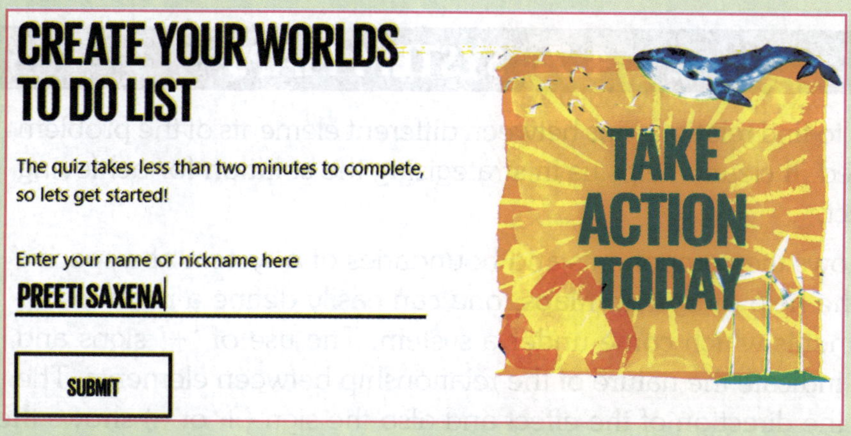

3. Click submit button and then play the interesting quiz.

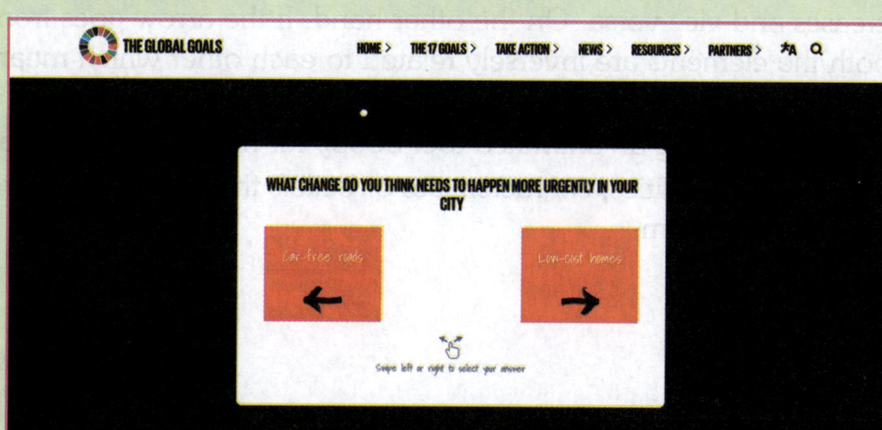

4.6.5 Why is Systems Thinking Important?

- Helps us **understand complex problems**.
- Makes us think about all the **long-term effects**, not just short-term.
- Teaches us to find **better solutions** by looking at the **whole picture**.

System Thinking is an approach that views problems as parts of an **interconnected whole** rather than isolated events. It asks:

- What elements completely make up the system?
- How do they interact through feedback loops?
- Where are power points where small changes yield big results?

4.6.6 Why Systems Thinking Helps

Complex problems like **climate change** or **urban poverty** are made up of many different factors that influence each other. For example, climate change involves pollution, deforestation, energy use, and even economic systems; all of that impact the environment in different ways. Similarly, urban poverty is driven by a mix of housing, education, jobs, healthcare, and more.

Systems thinking helps us understand these connections. Instead of trying to fix just one small part of the problem with a quick fix (the "silver bullet"), it shows us the root causes of issues and how they are all connected. This approach helps us avoid making things worse by fixing only one part without considering the bigger picture. By seeing how different parts interact, we can actually find better solutions that address the problem as a whole, leading to more lasting and effective change.

4.7 SYSTEM MAPS

System Maps help us to find relationships between different elements of the problem which we have scoped. It clearly helps us in strategizing the solution for achieving the goal of our project.

Treasure Link
NCASE LOOPY
in Action

Scan QR Code

A system map shows the components and boundaries of a system at a specific point in time. With the help of System Maps, one can easily define a relationship amongst several elements which come under a system. The use of '+' signs and '–' signs in the loops indicate the nature of the relationship between elements. The arrow- head depicts the direction of the effect and also the sign (+ or –) shows their relationship. If the arrow goes from X to Y with a + sign, it means that both are directly related to each other. That is, If X increases, Y also increases and vice versa. On the other hand, If the arrow goes from X to Y with a (–) sign, it means that both the elements are inversely related to each other which means if X increases, Y would decrease and vice-versa.

An example of system map using an animated tool Loopy for making System Map:

IDENTITY chart tells us the qualities, characteristics or beliefs that make a person who they are and also how does the world look at them.

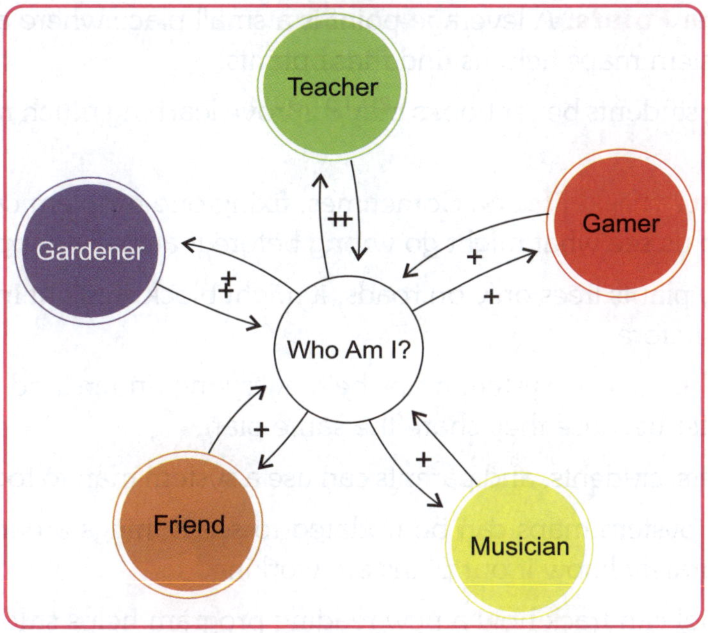

The **NCASE LOOPY** tool is an interactive online platform designed to help users visualize and fully understand complex systems through causal loop diagrams. Developed by Nicky Case, LOOPY allows you to create system maps by connecting variables with arrows to represent cause-and-effect relationships. These connections can thereby form feedback loops, which are central to systems thinking.

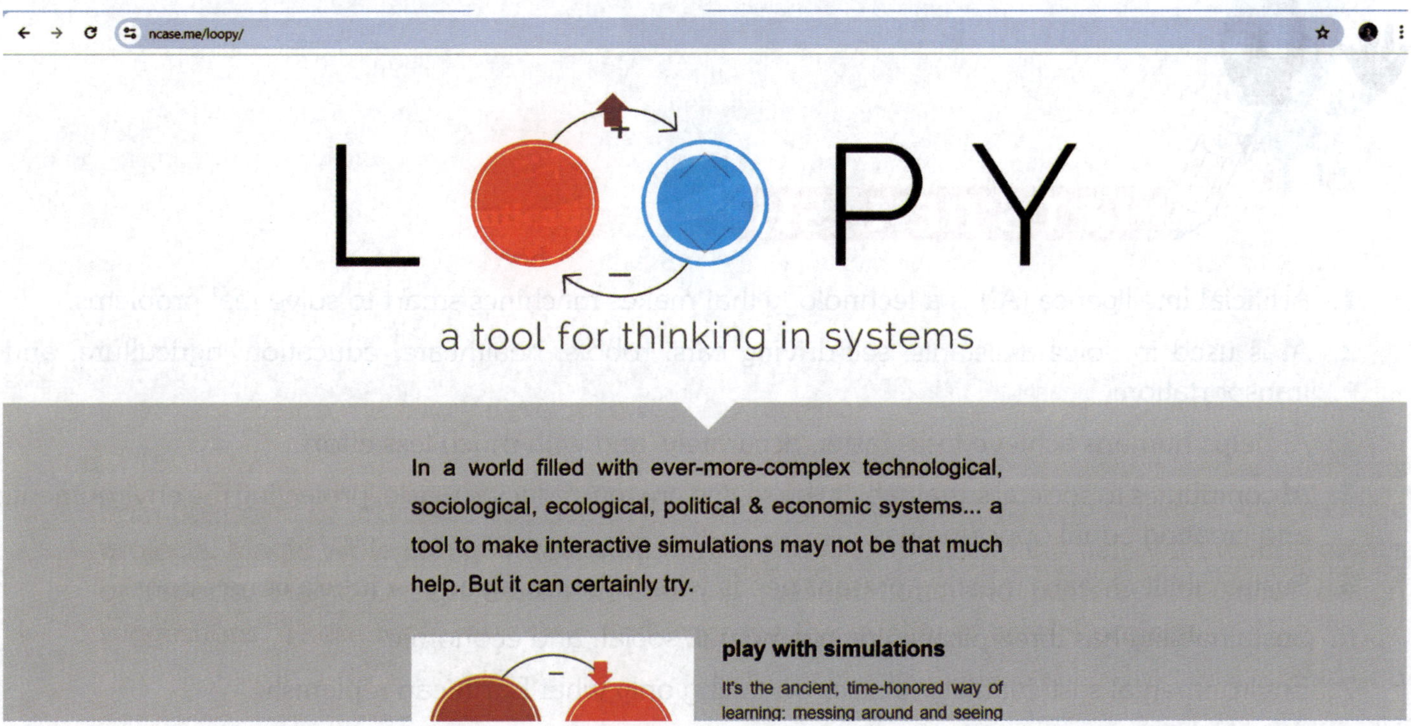

4.7.1 Purpose of System Maps

1. **Reveal Connections:** System maps show how different things are linked. Some connections are hidden, and the map then makes them clear.

   Example: In a school, better teaching helps students learn, that makes parents happy, and the school gets a better reputation.

2. **Identify Leverage Points:** A leverage point is a small place where a small change can make a big difference. System maps help us find these points.

   Example: Giving students better books may improve learning much more than just building new classrooms.

3. **Anticipate Unintended Effects:** Sometimes, fixing one problem can cause another problem. System maps help us see what might go wrong before it actually happens.

   Example: If a city plants trees only on roads, it might block sunlight in gardens, this is something we didn't think of before.

4. **Facilitate Collaboration:** System maps help everyone understand the same thing. Teams can work together better because they share the same plan.

   Example: Teachers, students, and parents can use a system map to together plan a school project

5. **Track Progress:** System maps can be updated to see if things are improving or getting worse. They help us accurately know if our plans are working.

   Example: A school can track how a new reading program helps students improve over a year.

Think of a system map like a "treasure map" for solving problems. It exactly shows where things are connected, where to focus, what might go wrong, and how to check if you're on the right path.

LET'S REHASH

1. Artificial Intelligence (AI) is a technology that makes machines smart to solve real problems.
2. AI is used in voice assistants, self-driving cars, robots, healthcare, education, agriculture, and transportation.
3. AI helps humans achieve tasks faster, accurately, and with much less effort.
4. AI contributes to societal sustainability by saving energy, reducing waste, protecting the environment, and creating equal opportunities.
5. Sustainability means meeting present needs without harming any of future generations.
6. Sustainability has three pillars: environmental, social, and economic.
7. Environmental sustainability focuses on taking only what Earth can replenish.
8. Social sustainability ensures all people live healthy, safe, and fair lives.
9. Economic sustainability means earning money in ways that can last for many years.
10. Sustainable Development Goals (SDGs) were adopted by the UN in back in the year 2015.
11. There are 17 SDGs addressing poverty, hunger, health, education, gender, energy, jobs, innovation, climate, and partnerships.

12. Systems thinking is looking at the whole system, understanding how parts are connected, and also seeing long-term effects.
13. A system is a group of parts working together to achieve a common purpose.
14. Important features of systems thinking include interconnections, feedback loops, delays, and no matter how small changes, causing unforeseen big effects.
15. System maps visually show relationships between elements of a system.
16. Arrows in system maps indicate direction of effect; + means direct relationship, it means inverse relationship.
17. Purposes of system maps include revealing connections, identifying leverage points, anticipating unintended effects, facilitating collaboration, and tracking progress.
18. System thinking helps in clearly understanding complex problems like climate change and urban poverty.
19. System maps act like a "treasure map" to show what affects the system, where to focus, and what might go wrong.
20. Tools like NCASE Loopy effectively help create interactive system maps and visualize feedback loops.

To Solve Multiple Choice Questions Online

Scan QR Code and Check Your Score

EXERCISE

A. Multiple Choice Questions with Answers

1. What is AI primarily used for?

(a) Only for making robots
(b) Making machines smarter, in order to solve complex problems
(c) Cleaning the environment (d) Playing games only

2. Which of the following is a pillar of sustainability?

(a) Social (b) Artificial
(c) Technological (d) Digital

3. Which SDG basically focuses on ending hunger?

(a) No Poverty (b) Zero Hunger
(c) Climate Action (d) Quality Education

4. Systems thinking helps us:

(a) Focus on one part only (b) See the whole system
(c) Ignore feedback loops (d) Work randomly

5. **Which symbol in a system map shows an inverse relationship?**
   (a) + (b) –
   (c) → (d) *

6. **AI can actually help societal sustainability by:**
   (a) Reducing waste (b) Increasing pollution
   (c) Making people lazy (d) None of these

7. **Economic sustainability ensures:**
   (a) Jobs and income that last (b) Only profit
   (c) Only nature protection (d) Ignoring resources

8. **Which tool is generally used to create system maps interactively?**
   (a) MS Word (b) NCASE Loopy
   (c) Excel (d) Google Maps

9. **A system is:**
   (a) A single object (b) A group of parts working together
   (c) Only a machine (d) A software program

10. **Which SDG ensures access to clean water?**
   (a) Clean Water & Sanitation (b) Affordable Energy
   (c) All Decent Work (d) Life on Land

11. **Small changes in a system can:**
   (a) Have no effect (b) Cause big effects
   (c) Slow down the system (d) Break the system only

12. **Which SDG is about climate action?**
   (a) SDG 13 (b) SDG 7
   (c) SDG 5 (d) SDG 12

13. **Interconnections in systems thinking truly mean:**
   (a) Parts are independent (b) Parts are linked
   (c) Parts are useless (d) Parts do not matter

14. **Feedback loops mean:**
   (a) Results come back as effects (b) Results disappear
   (c) Effects are ignored (d) Only money matters

15. **Sustainability is actually quite important because:**
   (a) Resources are unlimited (b) Ensures enough resources for all
   (c) Short-term profit matters only (d) People can waste freely

16. **Which SDG focuses on gender equality?**
   (a) SDG 2 (b) SDG 5
   (c) SDG 10 (d) SDG 7

17. System maps help in:

(a) Hiding relationships
(b) Revealing connections
(c) Ignoring problems
(d) Making random decisions

18. Delays in any systems mean:

(a) Effects are immediate
(b) Results take time
(c) Changes are useless
(d) Changes are ignored

19. Who developed the Loopy tool?

(a) Elon Musk
(b) Nicky Case
(c) Bill Gates
(d) Mark Zuckerberg

20. Which SDG promotes all partnerships for achieving goals?

(a) SDG 17
(b) SDG 12
(c) SDG 3
(d) SDG 7

ANSWERS

1.	(b)	2.	(a)	3.	(b)	4.	(b)	5.	(b)
6.	(a)	7.	(a)	8.	(b)	9.	(b)	10.	(a)
11.	(b)	12.	(a)	13.	(b)	14.	(a)	15.	(b)
16.	(b)	17.	(b)	18.	(b)	19.	(b)	20.	(a)

B. Fill in the Blanks with Answers

1. AI stands for __________.

Ans. Artificial Intelligence

2. Sustainability truly ensures meeting today's needs without harming __________.

Ans. future generations

3. The three pillars of sustainability are __________.

Ans. environmental, social, and economic

4. __________ is the SDG that aims to end hunger.

Ans. Zero Hunger

5. Systems thinking implies looking at the __________.

Ans. whole system

6. A system map shows __________.

Ans. relationships between different elements

7. In system maps, a + sign indicates a __________.

Ans. direct relationship

8. In system maps, a – sign indicates a __________.

Ans. inverse relationship

9. __________ is a tool that creates interactive system maps.

Ans. NCASE Loopy

10. __________ is SDG number 13.

Ans. Climate Action

11. __________ show that actions can come back as effects.

Ans. Feedback loops

12. Economic sustainability focuses on __________.

Ans. jobs and money that last

13. Social sustainability ensures everyone has __________.

Ans. health, safety, and fairness

14. AI can help __________.

Ans. save energy and reduce waste

15. System thinking teaches us to ably consider __________.

Ans. long-term effects

C. True & False

1. AI is only used for playing games.
2. Sustainability has three pillars: environmental, social, and economic.
3. A system is actually a group of unrelated parts.
4. Small changes in a system can create big effects.
5. Feedback loops mean that results do not affect the system.
6. System maps help in identifying connections and planning better.
7. Economic sustainability ignores money and jobs.
8. SDG 6 largely focuses on Clean Water and Sanitation.
9. Systems thinking focuses only on one part of a system.
10. NCASE Loopy is used to visualize system maps.

ANSWERS

1. False	**2.** True	**3.** False	**4.** True	**5.** False
6. True	**7.** False	**8.** True	**9.** False	**10.** True

D. Short Questions with Answers

1. What is Artificial Intelligence?

Ans. AI is a technology which makes machines smart to solve real problems.

2. Name the three pillars of sustainability.

Ans. Environmental, social, and economic.

3. Give an example of a system.

Ans. Human body – heart, lungs, stomach, and brain work together.

4. What is commonly known as systems thinking?

Ans. Systems thinking is understanding the whole system, its connections, and long-term effects.

5. What does a + sign in a system map indicate?

Ans. A direct relationship where one element increases, the other also increases.

6. Name any two fields where AI innovations are useful.

Ans. Healthcare and education (also agriculture, transportation).

7. What is the purpose of SDGs?

Ans. To achieve peace, prosperity, and sustainability for all by 2030.

8. What is a leverage point in a given system map?

Ans. A place where a small change can cause a big positive effect.

9. Why is systems thinking important for climate change?

Ans. It helps understand how pollution, deforestation, energy use, and economics are connected.

10. Give one relevant example of an unintended effect in system thinking.

Ans. Planting trees only on roads might block sunlight in gardens.

ACTIVITY-BASED QUESTIONS

1. **AI & Sustainability Game:**
   - Visit https://go-goals.org/
   - Download the game and play **two games** to see how many SDGs you can achieve.
2. Create a system map of your **school** showing connections between teachers, students, books, and playgrounds.
3. **Identify SDGs in Daily Life:** Make a list of **5 actions at home or school** that usually relate to any SDG (like saving water, planting trees, or using clean energy).
4. **Feedback Loop Exercise:** Take one activity (like studying) and draw a **feedback loop** showing how good results encourage more study and better grades.
5. Choose one SDG and sketch a mini system map showing at least three of the factors that reinforce or balance progress toward that goal. Where do you see the strongest influential point?

TEACHER'S NOTES

ACTIVITY

1. Play the **Go Goals! SDG** game online to explore Sustainable Development Goals.
2. Create a **system map** of the school showing connections between teachers, students, and resources.
3. List five daily actions that align with SDGs (e.g., saving water, planting trees).

EXPLANATION

Promote systems thinking and sustainability awareness. Guide students to see how AI innovations can support environmental and social goals.

CHAPTER 5

DIGITAL CITIZENSHIP

Digital Citizenship
in Action

Scan QR Code

OBJECTIVES

TOPICS TO BE COVERED

- Introduction to Citizenship
- The Concept of Digital Citizenship
- Responsibility in Digistal Citizenship — Netiquette
- Digital Drama
- Do's and Don'ts of Online Communication
- Digital Footprints
- Cookies
- Cyber-Security

5.1 INTRODUCTION TO CITIZENSHIP

The concept of citizenship originated in **Ancient Greece**, where "citizens" were individuals who had the legal right to participate in the affairs of the state, such as voting and decision-making in the public assembly. Citizenship refers to a legal status and relationship between an individual and his country or state. A citizen is someone who legally belongs to his nation and is granted certain rights, such as the right to vote, getting the share of its assets and also responsibilities towards it, such as obeying the laws, by that nation.

Fig. 5.1 Citizenship

5.2 THE CONCEPT OF DIGITAL CITIZENSHIP

Today, with the growing use of the internet and digital devices, the society is entering the phase of digital citizenship. Digital citizenship ensures that individuals can navigate the digital world safely, ethically, and responsibly. It allows users to interact positively online and protect themselves from the risks associated with digital spaces.

Fig. 5.2 Digital Citizenship

Digital Citizenship refers to a responsible and appropriate use of technology and the internet. Just like it is important to be a responsible citizen in a physical community, it is equally important to be a responsible digital citizen. It involves understanding the rights, responsibilities, and ethical behaviour needed to participate safely and effectively in the digital world. It includes applying digital literacy skills in a way that respects others and follows ethical standards.

Digital Literacy provides the basic skills needed to use technology effectively. This includes understanding how to operate devices, navigate the internet, and use the digital tools.

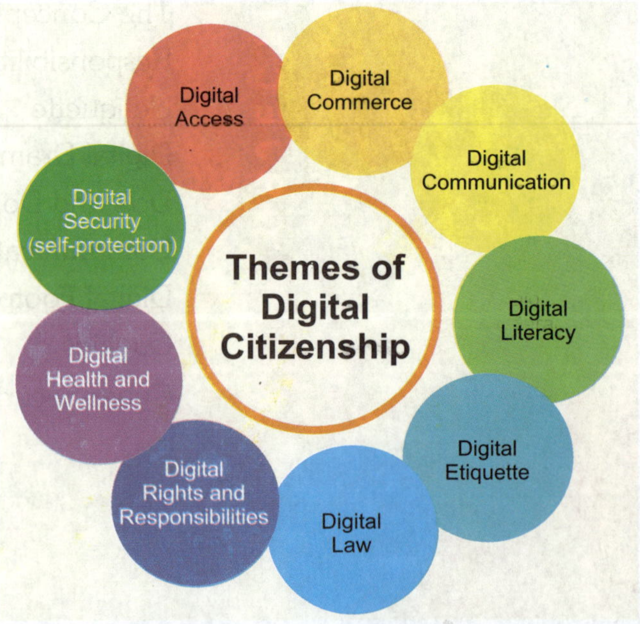

Fig. 5.3 Themes of Digital Citizenship

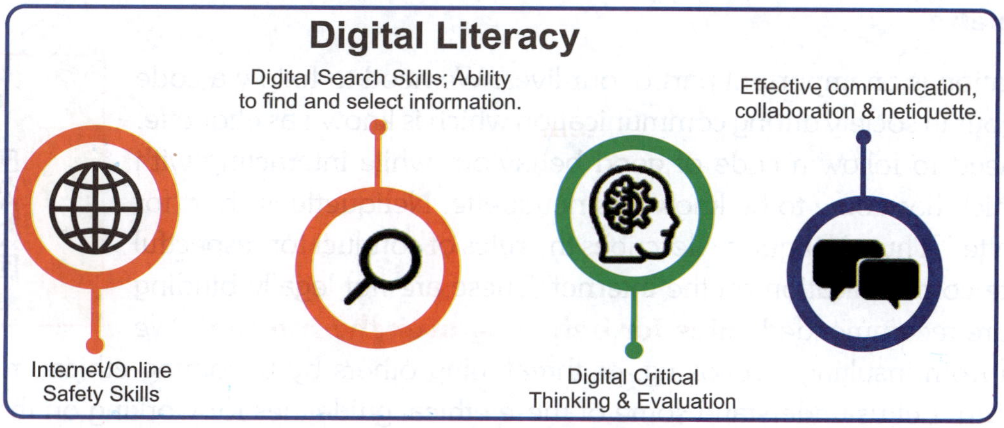

Fig. 5.4 Digital Literacy

5.3 RESPONSIBILITY IN DIGITAL CITIZENSHIP — NETIQUETTE

Today we have restricted ourselves to our smartphones. We work on the internet either through our devices or through our smartphones. Now we have become digital citizens. To become a responsible digital citizen, we need to follow the guidelines required for living in digital society. Let us first understand the meaning of etiquette.

Scooby-Doo Quest

Q. Name any 4 Digital Themes that are associated with Digital citizenship.

1. ____________ **2.** ____________

3. ____________ **4.** ____________

Answers: 1. Digital commerce **2.** Digital security **3.** Digital law **4.** Digital communication

Treasure Link
How to be a responsible Digital Citizen in Action

Scan QR Code

Fig. 5.5

K-Facts

Etiquette means following good manners and proper behaviour in different situations to show respect for others.

5.3.1 Netiquette

Treasure Link
Netiquette
in Action
Scan QR Code

Communication is an important part of our lives. We need to follow a code of polite behaviour in society during communication which is known as etiquette. Similarly, we need to follow a code of good behaviour while interacting with users online which has come to be known as netiquette. Netiquette is short for "Internet etiquette." Thus, Netiquette describes the rules of conduct for respectful and appropriate communication on the internet. These are not legally binding rules but they are recommended **rules for behaving over the internet**. We need to refrain from insulting, provoking, or threatening others by becoming ethical, respectful and a responsible citizen. Let us understand some of these ethical guidelines for working on the net.

8 tips to stay safe online

Fig. 5.6 8 tips to stay safe online

1. **Protect your privacy** online by using strong passwords, and avoid oversharing personal information. Also manage privacy settings to keep your account safe online.
2. **Stay safe online** and avoid clicking on any suspicious links. It is safer to use antivirus software and verify websites' authenticity before providing data.
3. **Respect others' opinion** and be kind during online communication. Avoid trolling and practise cultural sensitivity in online interactions.
4. **Think about the impact** of the information you post online. Never spread any misinformation on any digital platform and manage your digital footprint.
5. **Share your data responsibly** and respect copyrights rules. Avoid harmful content and give proper credit to creators.
6. **Report harmful content** and promote ethical behaviour within your online communities.

5.4 DIGITAL DRAMA

When we ignore the netiquettes, it gives rise to online disputes. These disputes are known as digital drama. Thus, digital drama refers to the everyday disputes that occur among friends or other acquaintances online. This could be in the form of hurtful comments, embarrassing photos, or inconsiderate rumours. In some cases, digital drama can grow up into an offline conflict — verbal or even physical. As a responsible digital citizen, always ask yourself these questions before posting anything online.

Fig. 5.7

5.5 DO'S AND DON'TS OF ONLINE COMMUNICATION

We should be careful while communicating online so it is better that we know the do's and don'ts of online communication.

Treasure Link
Netiquette (Do's and Dont's) in Action
Scan QR Code

Do's of online communication

1. Be respectful and polite in your tone when communicating with others.
2. Use clear and concise language to avoid misunderstanding.
3. Verify facts before sharing information to prevent spreading misinformation.
4. Protect your personal information and that of others by maintaining privacy.
5. Encourage positive and constructive discussions, and support diverse viewpoints.
6. Respond promptly to important messages and emails in a professional manner.

Don'ts of online communication

1. Don't use offensive language while communicating online.
2. Don't engage in cyberbullying.

Scooby-Doo Quest

Q. Write any 3 don'ts of online communication.

1. ________________
2. ________________
3. ________________

Answers: 1. Don't engage in cyberbullying **2.** Don't share sensitive information **3.** Don't use offensive language

3. Don't share sensitive information like passwords or financial details.
4. Don't post misleading or false information without checking facts.
5. Don't engage in online arguments or intensify conflicts unnecessarily.
6. Don't share content without the original creator's permission.
7. Don't fall for scams or phishing links, especially from unverified sources.

Fig. 5.8

5.6 DIGITAL FOOTPRINTS

We browse internet for various reasons, such as searching information, for submitting any information, for downloading any information online or for sending emails across various digital platforms. When we visit the internet on any site using any smart device like smartphone, tablet, laptop, desktop, etc., we leave a trail of data that reflects our online activities. This trail of data is known as Digital Footprints.

Treasure Link
Digital Footprint in Action
Scan QR Code

In short, digital footprints show our day-to-day activities that we do on the internet like the site we visit, emails we send, and any information we submit online. A digital footprint is also known as a digital shadow or an electronic footprint. It includes websites we have visited along with our computer's IP address, location, and other device-specific details. As advancement in digital technology is increasing, our digital footprint is created in many ways like posting comments on social media, posting reels or uploading pictures/videos on social media, subscribing to a newsletter, leaving an online review, or shopping online. These footprints can be exploited for targeted advertisement or misused with any mal intention. We are living in the world of artificial intelligence, so companies are constantly looking for to trapping your data online. These companies can get access to your confidential personal data using these digital footprints. We all need to be aware that whatever we write or upload or post online should not be offensive or annoying to anyone or that can harm us in any way.

Digital Footprints are of two types:

1. Active footprints.
2. Passive footprints.

1. **Active footprints:** Active footprints are those data trails that are intentionally left by users online; these include data that we intentionally submit online or that we share online in the form of social media posts, likes, sharing, and comments, blog posts that are published online, reviews and ratings on products, services, or businesses, email communication, etc.
2. **Passive footprints:** Passive footprints are those data trails that are made by the user on the internet unintentionally. These include the data generated automatically when the user browses the internet, searches data online, visit websites, do online purchasing and other similar online activities. Passive footprints are harder to track and manage because they can be collected without user consent.

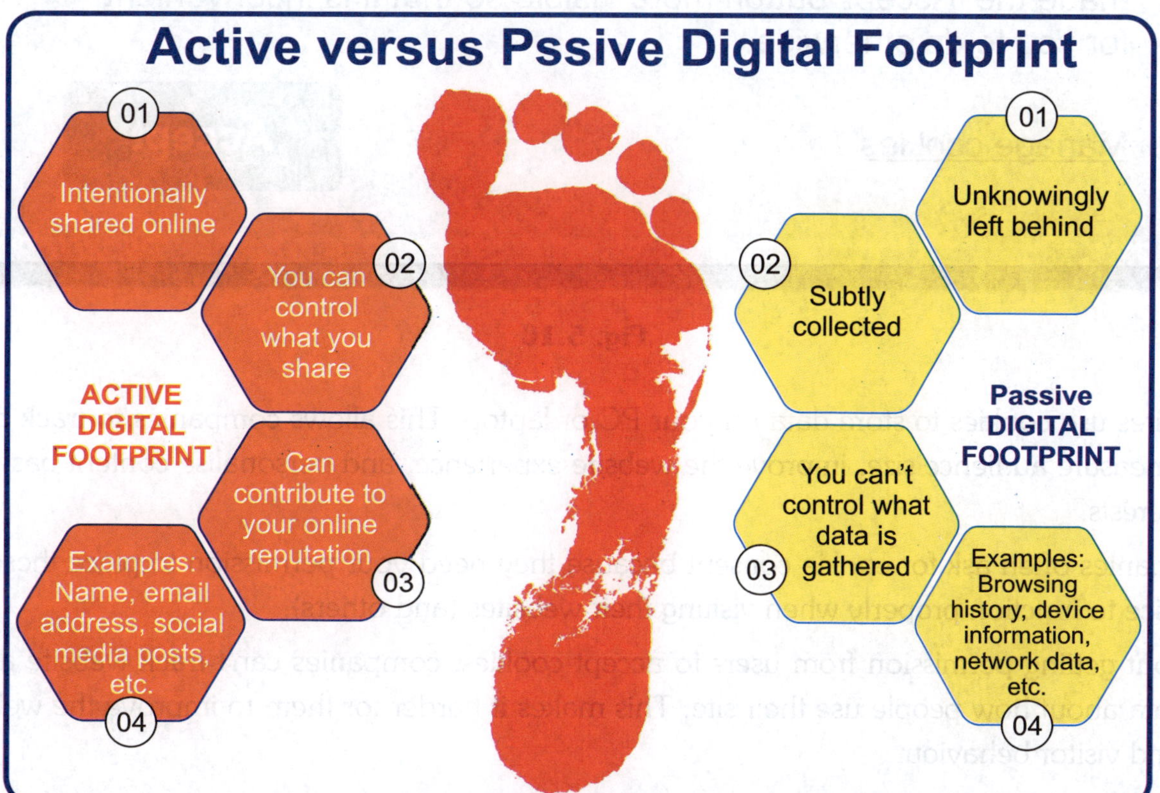

Fig. 5.9 Active Versus Passive Digital Footprint

We may not have power to remove or erase that data, neither do we have any control on how that data will be used. This means that once a data trail is generated, our digital footprints will remain there even if we try to erase data about our online activities later. We cannot guarantee complete removal of data footprints. Therefore, we need to be very cautious while working online. Since all our online activities leave a data trace on the Internet and even on the computing device, they can be used to track the user, their location, device and other usage details.

5.7 COOKIES

Cookies are small text files stored on your device by websites which you visit. They help those websites to remember information about the your visit, such as login details, preferences, or items in a shopping cart. This enables a more personalised user experience. Cookies can also track user activity for analytics and advertising purposes. Cookies don't contain viruses, but they can slow down your device and drain its battery life by downloading resources from the web server while browsing.

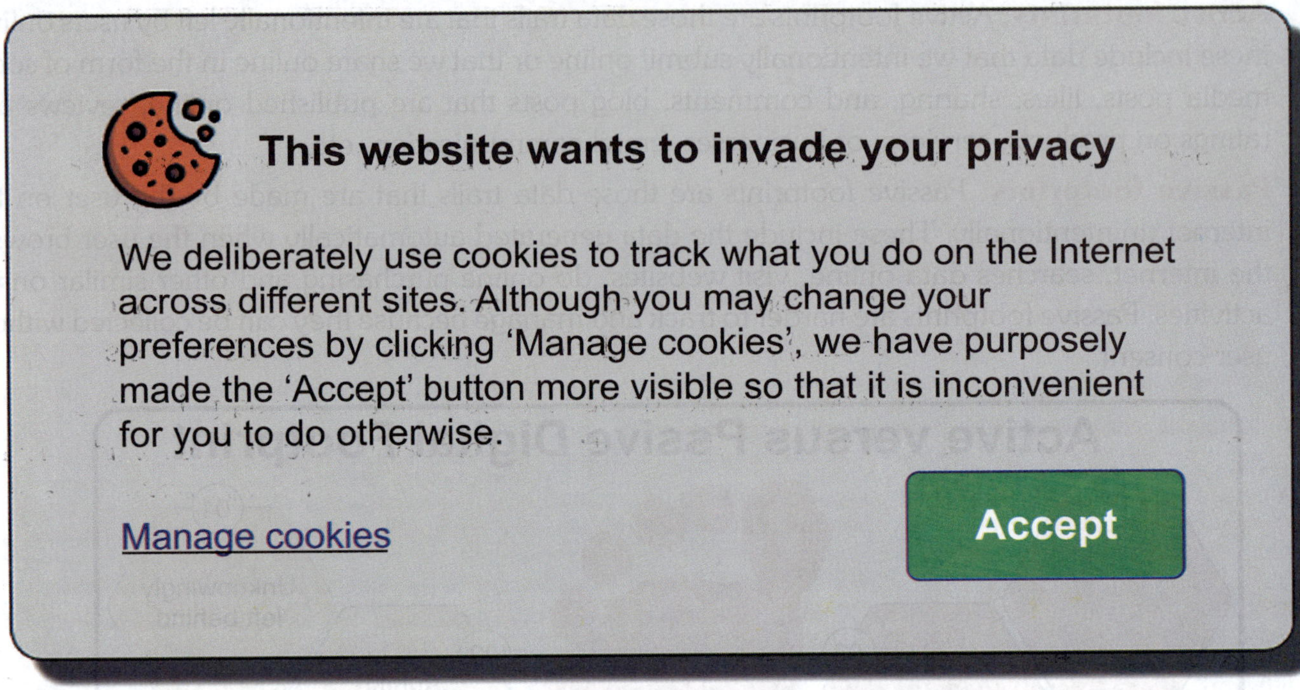

Fig. 5.10

Websites use cookies to store data on your PC or laptop. This allows companies to track the user's activity, measure audience size, improve the website experience, and personalise content based on the user's interests.

Companies often ask for cookie consent because they need your permission to place these files on your device to function properly when visiting their websites (and others).

Without getting permission from users to accept cookies, companies can't track website activity or collect data about how people use their site. This makes it harder for them to improve the website and understand visitor behaviour.

5.8 CYBER SECURITY

Cyber Security is the practice of protecting computers, networks, and data from attacks, theft, or damage by hackers or viruses. Just like locking your house keeps your belongings safe, Cyber Security uses tools like passwords, antivirus software, and firewalls to keep information safe online. It helps to protect personal details, such as passwords, photos, and bank information, and keeps websites and apps running smoothly without being harmed by cybercriminals. It is important for everyone to be careful online and learn how to stay safe, such as by **not** sharing private information or clicking on suspicious links.

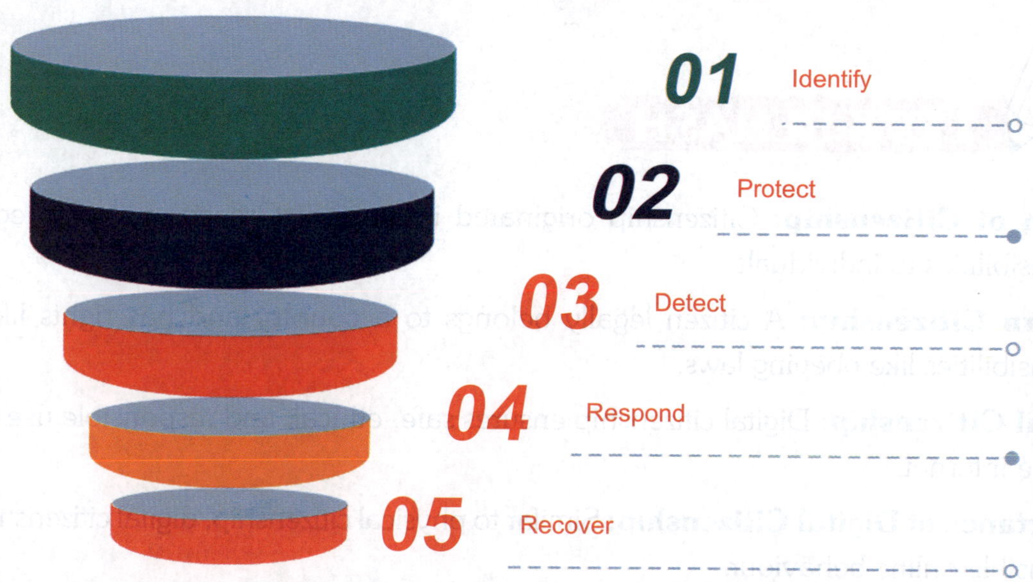

Fig. 5.11 5 Key Elements of Cyber Security

We can ensure Cyber Security by following a few important steps:

1. **Use strong passwords:** Create passwords that are hard to guess, with a mix of letters, numbers, and symbols, and avoid using the same password for multiple accounts.
2. **Enable two-factor authentication (2FA):** This adds an extra layer of security by requiring a second step to log in, like a code sent to your phone.

Treasure Link
Cyber Security Awareness for Kids
in Action
Scan QR Code

3. **Keep software updated:** Regularly update your operating system, apps, and antivirus software to protect against the newly developed security threats.
4. **Be cautious of suspicious links and emails:** Don't click on links or download attachments from unknown or untrusted sources, as they may contain malware.
5. **Use antivirus and firewall protection:** These tools help to detect and block harmful threats like viruses and hackers.
6. **Back up your data:** Regularly save important files at a separate and secure place so that you don't lose them in case of an attack.
7. **Be mindful of public Wi-Fi:** Avoid using public networks for sensitive tasks, or use a Virtual Private Network (VPN) to protect your data.

LET'S REHASH

1. **Origin of Citizenship:** Citizenship originated in Ancient Greece, granting legal rights and responsibilities to individuals.
2. **Modern Citizenship:** A citizen legally belongs to a country and has rights like voting and responsibilities like obeying laws.
3. **Digital Citizenship:** Digital citizenship ensures safe, ethical, and responsible use of technology and the internet.
4. **Importance of Digital Citizenship:** Similar to physical citizenship, digital citizenship emphasizes responsible online behaviour.
5. **Digital Literacy:** Ability to understand and effectively use technology and the internet. This is essential for digital citizens.
6. **Becoming a Responsible Digital Citizen:** Adherance to laid out guidelines and good practices online. This helps individuals to act responsibly in the digital world.
7. **Netiquette:** Netiquette refers to adopting the rules of respectful conduct during online interactions.
8. **Protect Privacy:** Use strong passwords and judicious sharing of personal information online.
9. **Stay Safe Online:** Avoid clicking on suspicious links and use antivirus software to secure your devices.
10. **Respect Others:** Be respectful during online conversations, avoiding trolling or harassment.
11. **Digital Drama:** Digital drama arises from online disputes, often due to ignoring netiquette.
12. **Do's of Online Communication:** Be polite, clear, fact-check, protect privacy, and encourage constructive discussions.
13. **Don'ts of Online Communication:** Avoid offensive language, cyberbullying, sharing sensitive information, and spreading false information.
14. **Digital Footprints:** Online activities leave a trail of data that shows what users do on the internet.
15. **Active Footprints:** Active digital footprints are created intentionally through social media posts, comments, and online reviews.
16. **Passive Footprints:** Passive footprints are created unintentionally through browsing and online searches.
17. **Cookies:** Cookies are small files stored on your device by many websites to enhance user experience and track activity.

18. **Cyber Security:** Cyber Security protects computers and data from threats using tools like passwords and antivirus software.
19. **Cyber Security Practices:** Using strong passwords, enabling two-factor authentication, keeping software updated, and avoiding suspicious links.
20. **Public Wi-Fi Caution:** Avoid using public networks for sensitive activities or use VPNs for added protection.

To Solve Multiple Choice Questions Online

Scan QR Code and Check Your Score

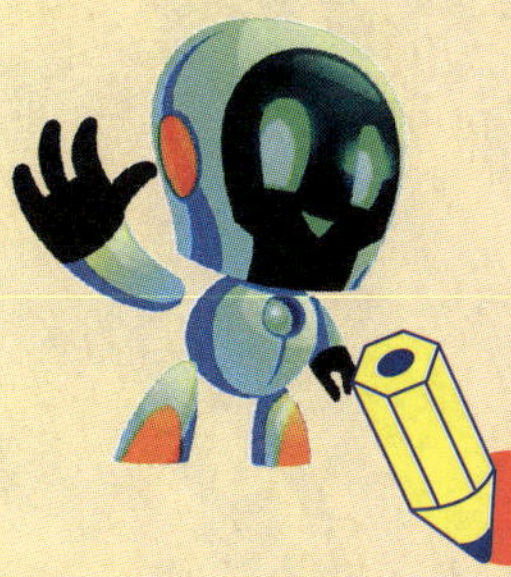

EXERCISE

A. Multiple Choice Questions with Answers

1. **Where did the concept of citizenship originate?**
   (a) Rome (b) Egypt
   (c) Greece (d) India
2. **What is digital citizenship?**
   (a) Using paper documents
   (b) Responsible use of technology and the internet
   (c) Voting in elections
   (d) Avoiding the internet
3. **What is netiquette?**
   (a) Internet speed
   (b) Polite online behaviour
   (c) Cybercrime
   (d) Using public Wi-Fi
4. **Which of the following is an example of active digital footprint?**
   (a) Browsing a website
   (b) Submitting an online review
   (c) Tracking cookies
   (d) Passive data collection

5. **What do cookies help websites in recording?**
   (a) Details of user's visit on their websites
   (b) Weather forecasts
   (c) User's files
   (d) Online security threats

6. **What is one way to protect your privacy online?**
   (a) Using a good firewall
   (b) Taking regular backups of your data
   (c) Using strong passwords
   (d) Using an antivirus software

7. **Digital literacy refers to:**
   (a) Writing documents by hand
   (b) Understanding and using technology effectively
   (c) Avoiding online platforms
   (d) Online gaming

8. **What is a passive digital footprint?**
   (a) Intentional social media posts
   (b) Unintentionally created through browsing
   (c) Physical paperwork
   (d) Deleted files

9. **Which of the following is NOT a part of Cyber Security?**
   (a) Using firewalls
   (b) Sharing passwords freely
   (c) Enabling two-factor authentication
   (d) Keeping software updated

10. **What is digital drama?**
   (a) An online play
   (b) Everyday online disputes
   (c) A website feature
   (d) Secure web browsing

11. **How can digital footprints be misused?**
   (a) For targeted advertisements
   (b) For writing blogs
   (c) For learning online
   (d) For playing games

12. **Which action is considered netiquette?**
   (a) Using offensive language
   (b) Respecting others' opinions online
   (c) Clicking on suspicious links
   (d) Ignoring people online

13. **What can digital footprints include?**
   (a) Social media posts and likes
   (b) Device passwords
   (c) Physical addresses
   (d) Real-time conversations

14. What should you NOT do during online communication?

(a) Be polite
(b) Engage in cyberbullying
(c) Verify facts
(d) Protect personal information

15. What is one way to ensure Cyber Security?

(a) Use weak passwords
(b) Click on every link
(c) Enable two-factor authentication
(d) Share personal information

16. What do cookies store?

(a) User's visit preferences
(b) Viruses
(c) Digital footprints
(d) Strong passwords

17. What does 2FA stand for in Cyber Security?

(a) Two-Factor Authentication
(b) Two-Factor Access
(c) Two-Face Authentication
(d) Total Factor Assurance

18. What is digital footprint also known as?

(a) Digital shadow
(b) Digital block
(c) Digital light
(d) Digital wall

19. Why do companies ask for cookie consent?

(a) To slow down your device
(b) To access private messages
(c) To track website activity and improve user experience
(d) To delete your data

20. What does Cyber Security protect against?

(a) Strong passwords
(b) Computer viruses
(c) Printed documents
(d) Public Wi-Fi

ANSWERS

1. (c)	2. (b)	3. (b)	4. (b)	5. (a)
6. (c)	7. (b)	8. (b)	9. (b)	10. (b)
11. (a)	12. (b)	13. (a)	14. (b)	15. (c)
16. (a)	17. (a)	18. (a)	19. (c)	20. (b)

B. Fill in the Blanks with Answers

1. Citizenship originated in Ancient ....

Ans. Greece

2. .... citizenship ensures that individuals act responsibly online.

Ans. Digital

3. Netiquette is the short form of Internet ....

Ans. etiquette

4. Using strong .... can protect your online accounts.

Ans. passwords

5. Digital drama refers to online .... among friends.

Ans. disputes

6. Digital footprints show our day-to-day .... online.

Ans. activities

7. Cookies store small .... files on your device.

Ans. text

8. .... footprints are intentionally left by users online.

Ans. Active

9. .... helps to protect computers and networks from attacks.

Ans. Cyber Security

10. Always enable .... for added security on your accounts.

Ans. two-factor authentication

11. Avoid clicking on .... links for better online safety.

Ans. suspicious

12. .... online behaviour is essential for good netiquette.

Ans. Respectful

13. .... footprints can be misused for targeted advertisements.

Ans. Digital

14. .... footprints are created unintentionally.

Ans. Passive

15. Before sharing, always verify .... to avoid spreading misinformation.

Ans. facts

16. Digital citizenship includes practising .... online.

Ans. ethics

17. .... are files that websites use to track user activity.

Ans. Cookies

18. Digital .... can sometimes escalate to offline conflicts.

Ans. drama

19. .... information should not be overshared online.

Ans. Personal

20. .... help to protect your computer from hackers.

Ans. Firewalls

C. Short Questions with Answers

1. What is digital citizenship?

Ans. Digital citizenship is the responsible and appropriate use of technology and the internet.

2. What is netiquette?

Ans. Netiquette refers to a code of polite and respectful behaviour while interacting online.

3. What are active digital footprints?

Ans. Active digital footprints are data trails intentionally left by users through social media posts, comments, and reviews.

4. What does Cyber Security aim to protect?

Ans. Cyber Security aims to protect computers, networks, and data from attacks or damage.

5. Why is two-factor authentication important?

Ans. Two-factor authentication adds an extra layer of security by requiring a second verification step.

6. What are cookies used for?

Ans. Cookies are used to store information about a user's visit to a website, helping in personalizing the experience.

7. What is digital drama?

Ans. Digital drama refers to online disputes or conflicts that occur between friends or acquaintances.

8. What is a passive digital footprint?

Ans. A passive digital footprint is created unintentionally through online activities like browsing and searching.

9. What should you do before posting online?

Ans. Before posting online, consider the impact of the post and ensure that it does not spread misinformation.

10. Why should you avoid using public Wi-Fi for sensitive tasks?

Ans. Public Wi-Fi is less secure, making it easier for hackers to access your information.

ACTIVITY-BASED QUESTIONS

1. **Create a Netiquette Poster:** Design a poster illustrating the key rules of netiquette. Use visuals and catchy phrases to highlight the importance of respectful online behaviour.
2. **Track Your Digital Footprint:** Over the course of a week, keep a journal of your online activities (websites visited, comments made, etc.). Reflect on how these activities contribute to your digital footprint and suggest ways to improve responsible online behaviour.

TEACHER'S NOTES

ACTIVITY

1. Design a **Netiquette Poster** illustrating rules for respectful online behavior.

2. Keep a **Digital Footprint Journal** for a week and reflect on responsible online behavior.

EXPLANATION

Encourage reflection on online ethics, safety, and digital responsibility. Discuss how digital footprints affect personal reputation and cybersecurity.

LEARN WITH AI

1. Watch this video and find what is AI:

Treasure Link
What is AI?
in Action

Scan QR Code

SIRI
ALEXA

2. Watch the video and learn about AI in detail.

Treasure Link
Learn About AI in Detail
in Action

Scan QR Code

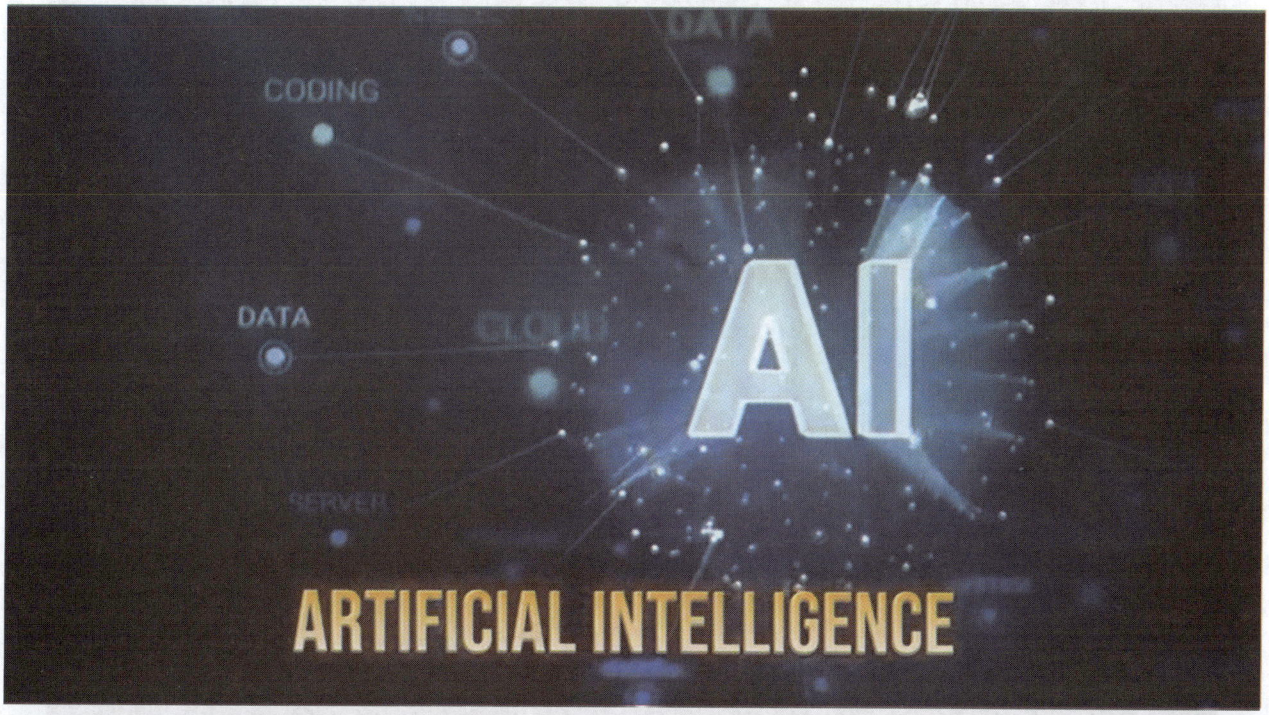

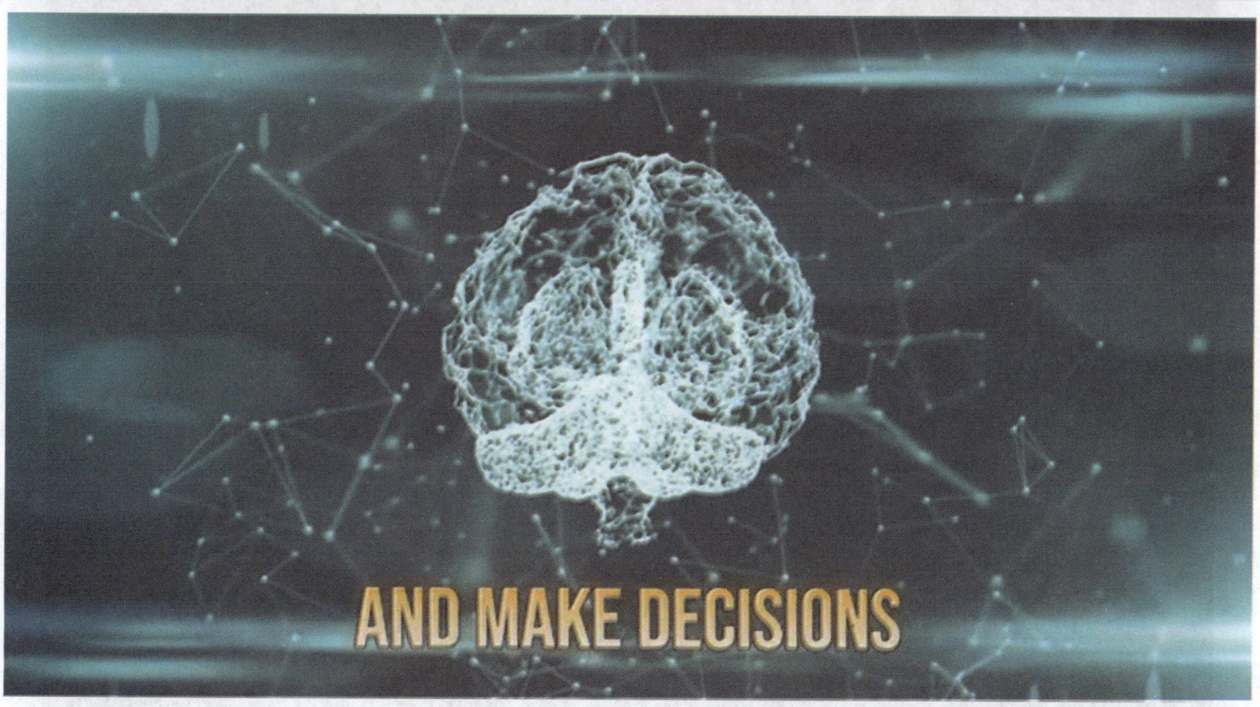

3. Watch and see How AI works:

Treasure Link
How AI works
in Action

Scan QR Code

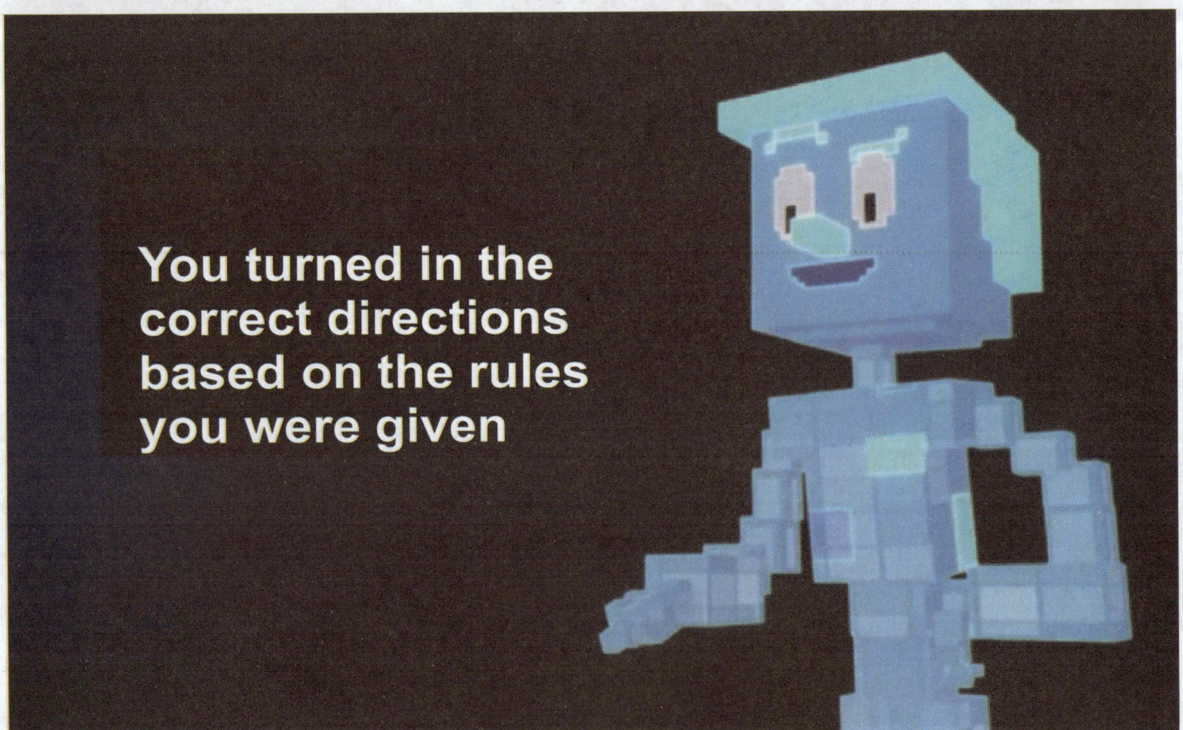

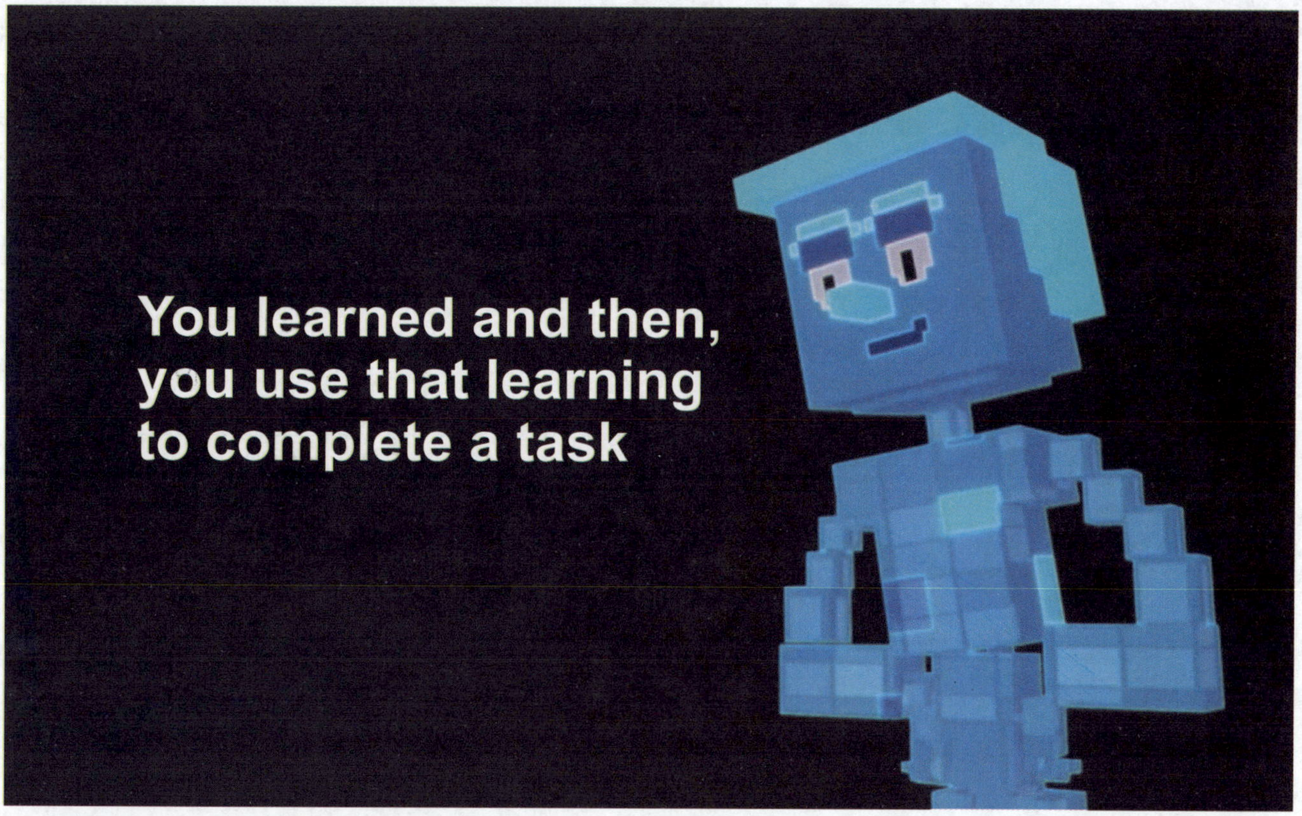

FUN.AI ACTIVITY

Treasure Link
Infinie Craft by Neal
in Action

Scan QR Code

1. **GAME:** Visit the site: https://neal.fun/infinite-craft/

Infinite Craft By Neal

<< An artificial intelligence game in which you have to combine two elements to create a new one.>>

Combine the elements by dragging so as to create another new element,such as combine water and fire to create steam.

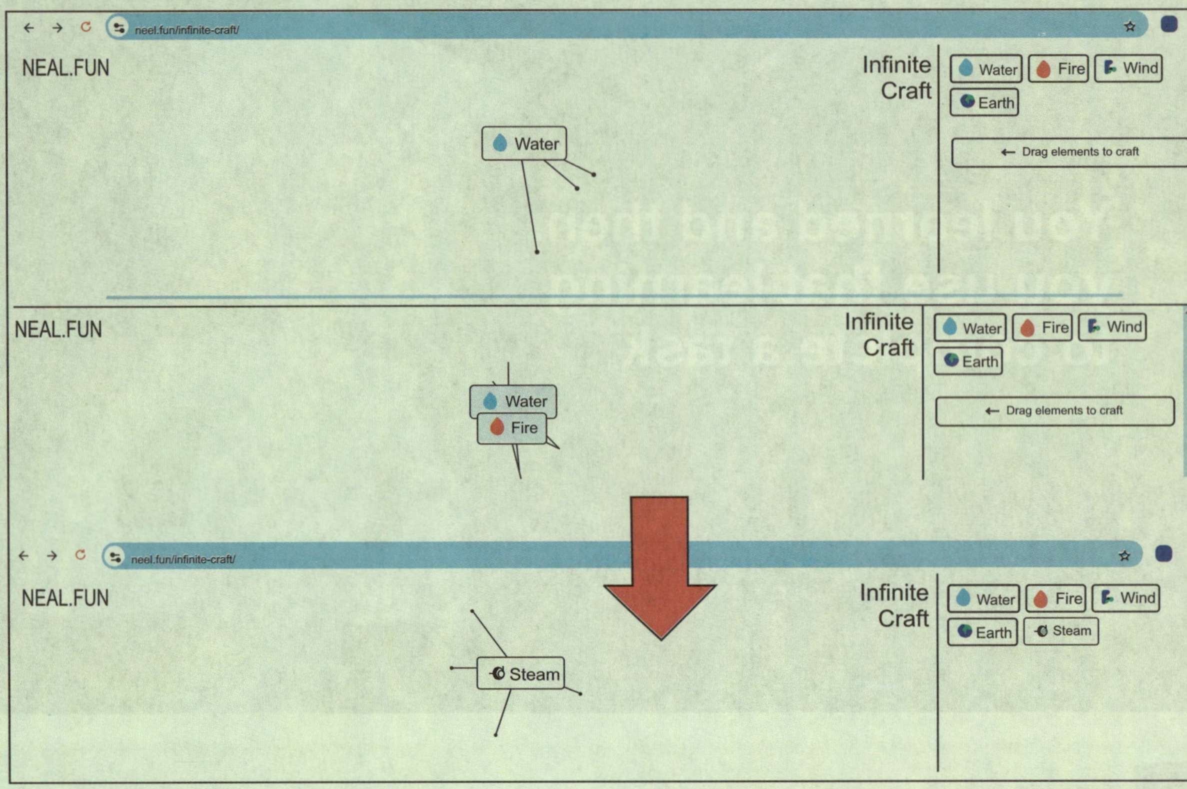

2. **GAME:** Visit the website given below and find whether the questions are replied by a bot or a human.
https://humanornot.so/

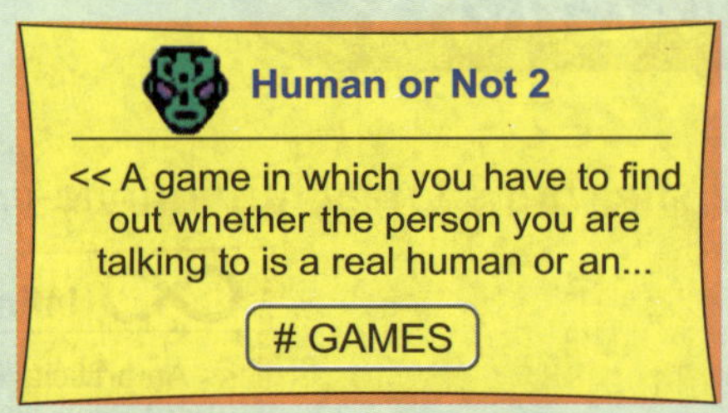

Treasure Link
Game 2
in Action

Scan QR Code

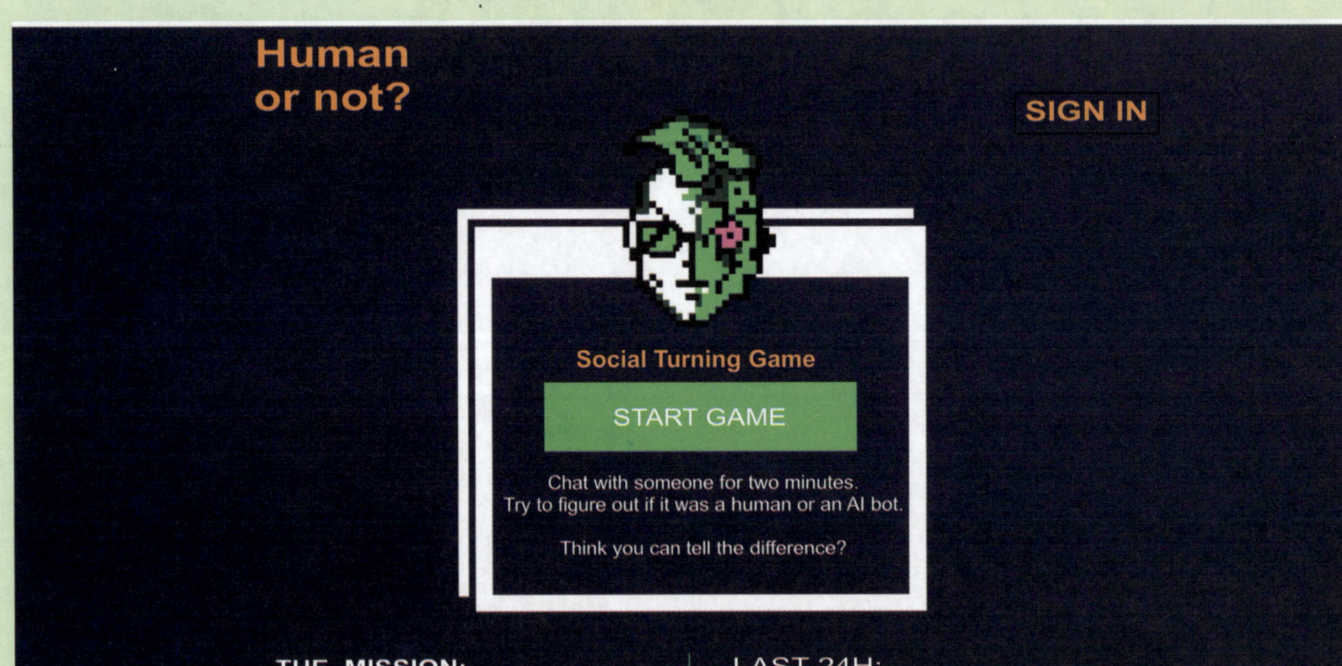

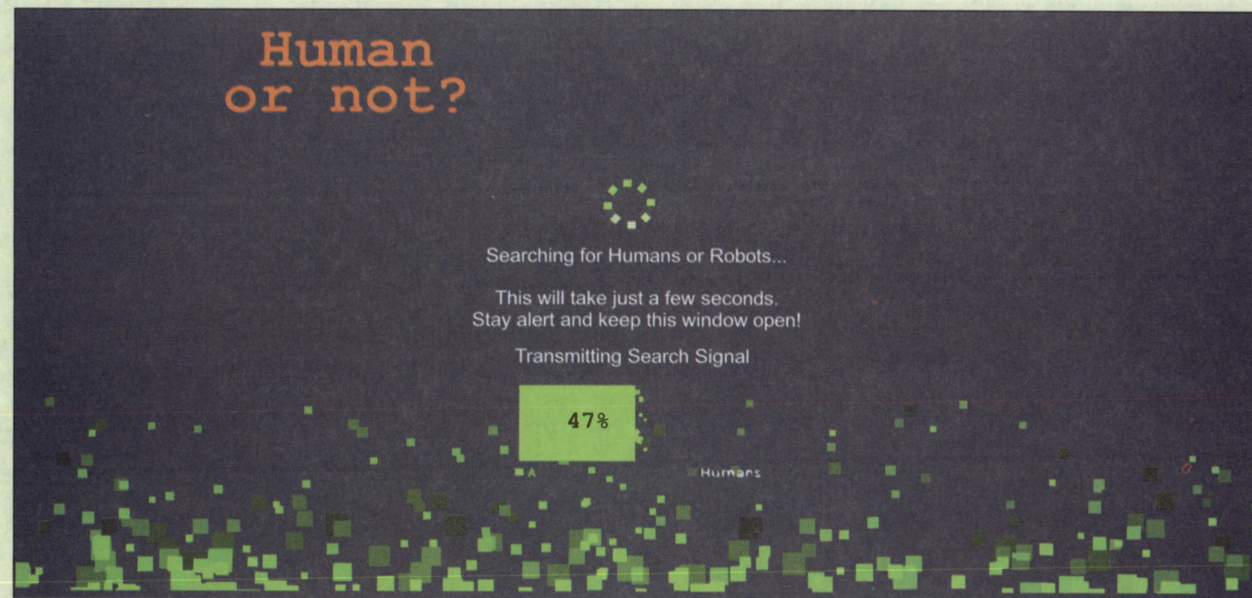
Human
or not?
Searching for Humans or Robots...
This will take just a few seconds.
Stay alert and keep this window open!
Transmitting Search Signal
47%
Humans

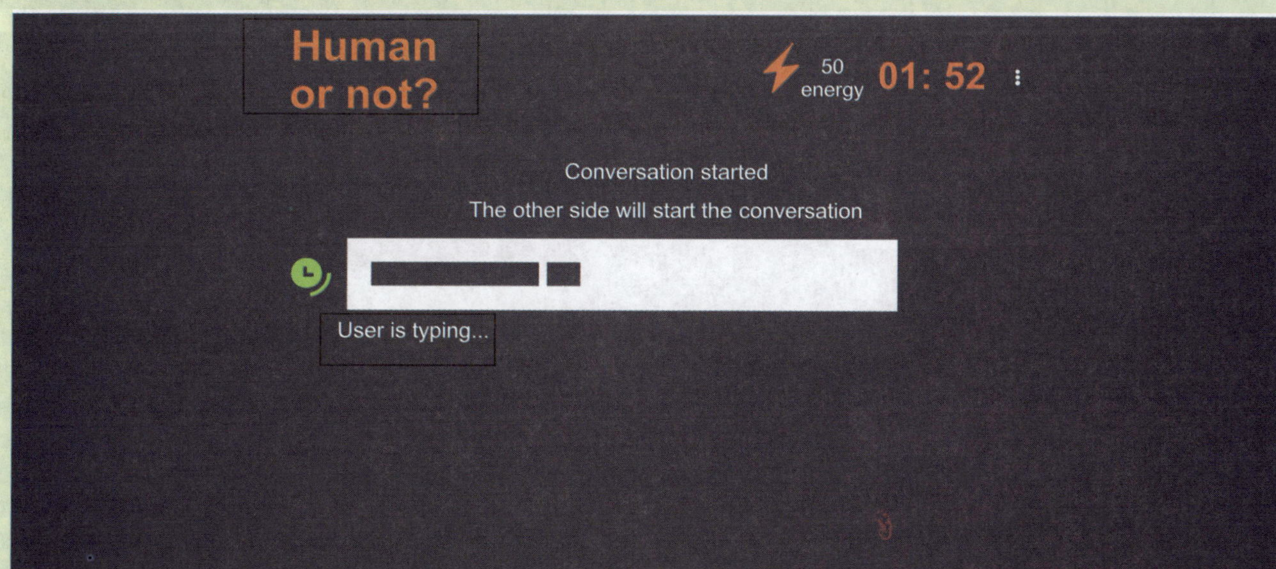
Human
or not?
50
energy
01: 52
Conversation started
The other side will start the conversation
User is typing...

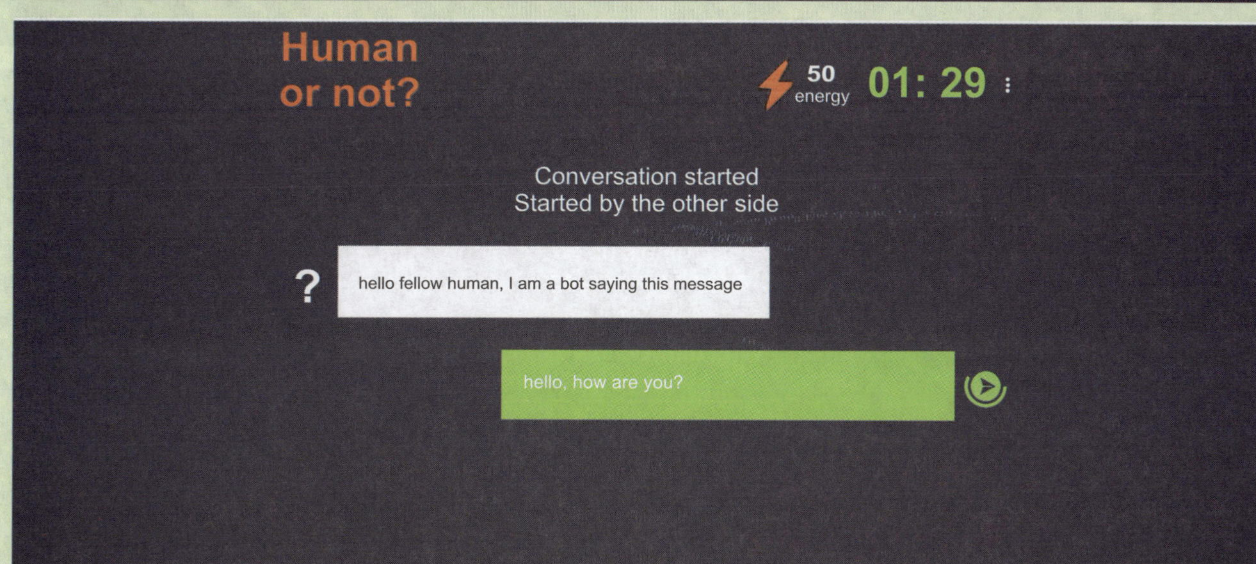
Human
or not?
50
energy
01: 29
Conversation started
Started by the other side
?
hello fellow human, I am a bot saying this message
hello, how are you?

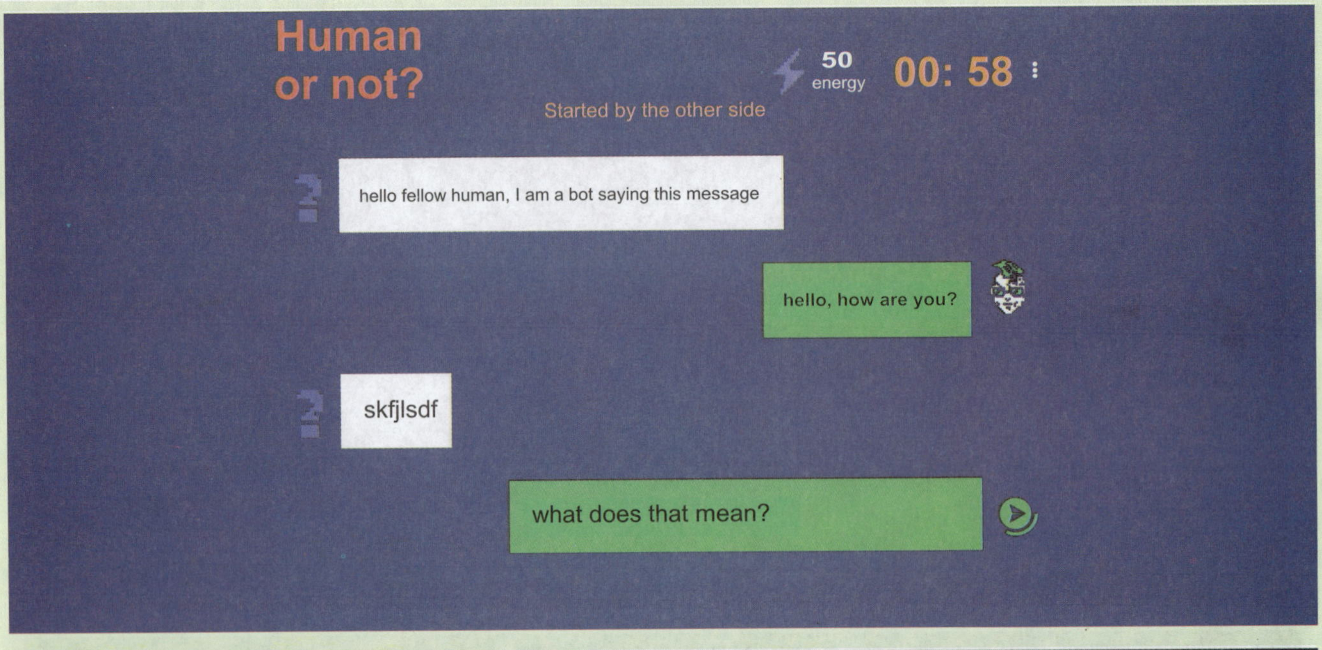
Human
or not?
50
energy
00: 58
Started by the other side
hello fellow human, I am a bot saying this message
hello, how are you?
skfjlsdf
what does that mean?

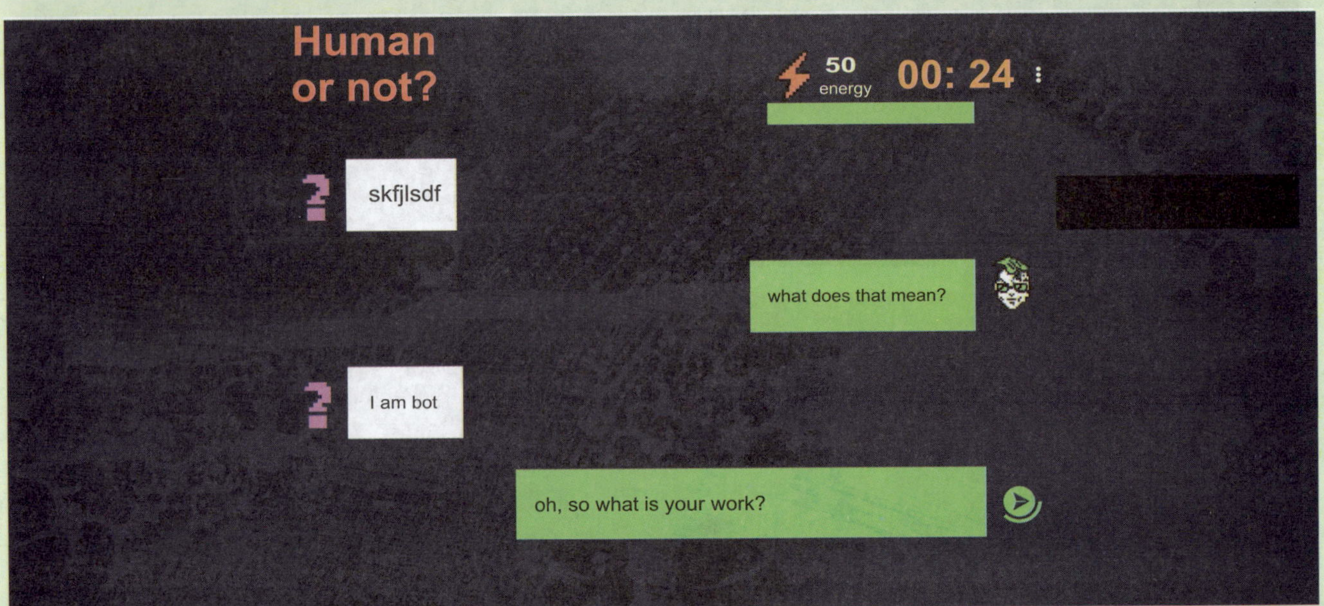
Human
or not?
50
energy
00: 24
skfjlsdf
what does that mean?
I am bot
oh, so what is your work?

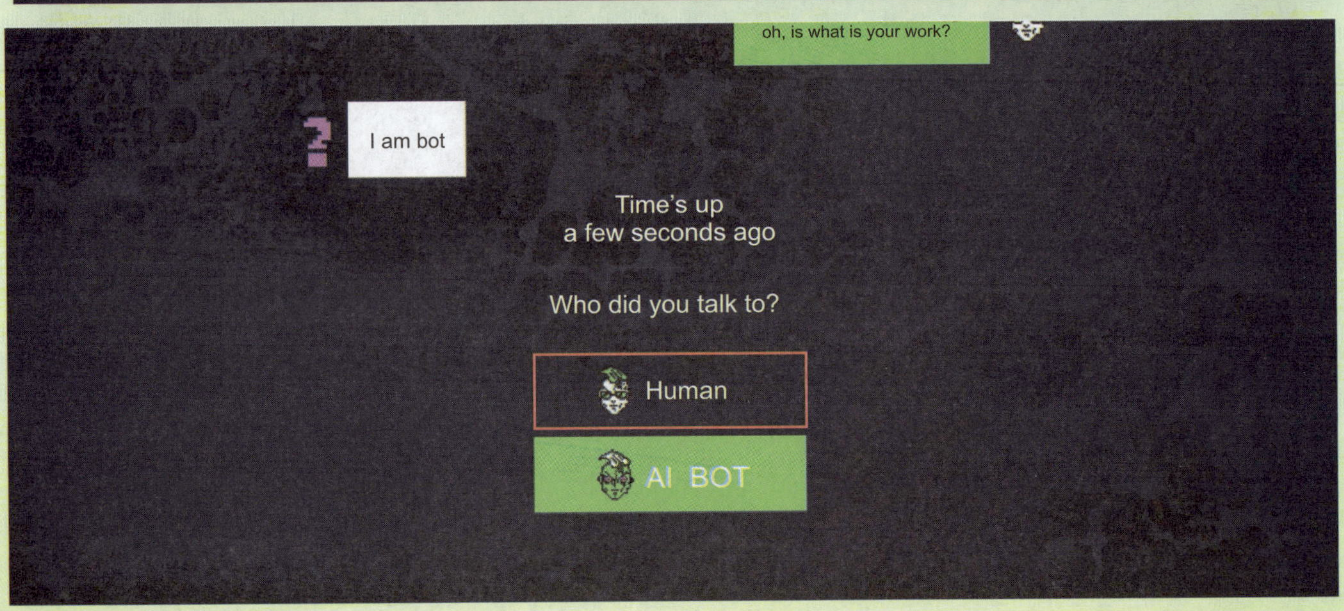
oh, is what is your work?
I am bot
Time's up
a few seconds ago
Who did you talk to?
Human
AI BOT

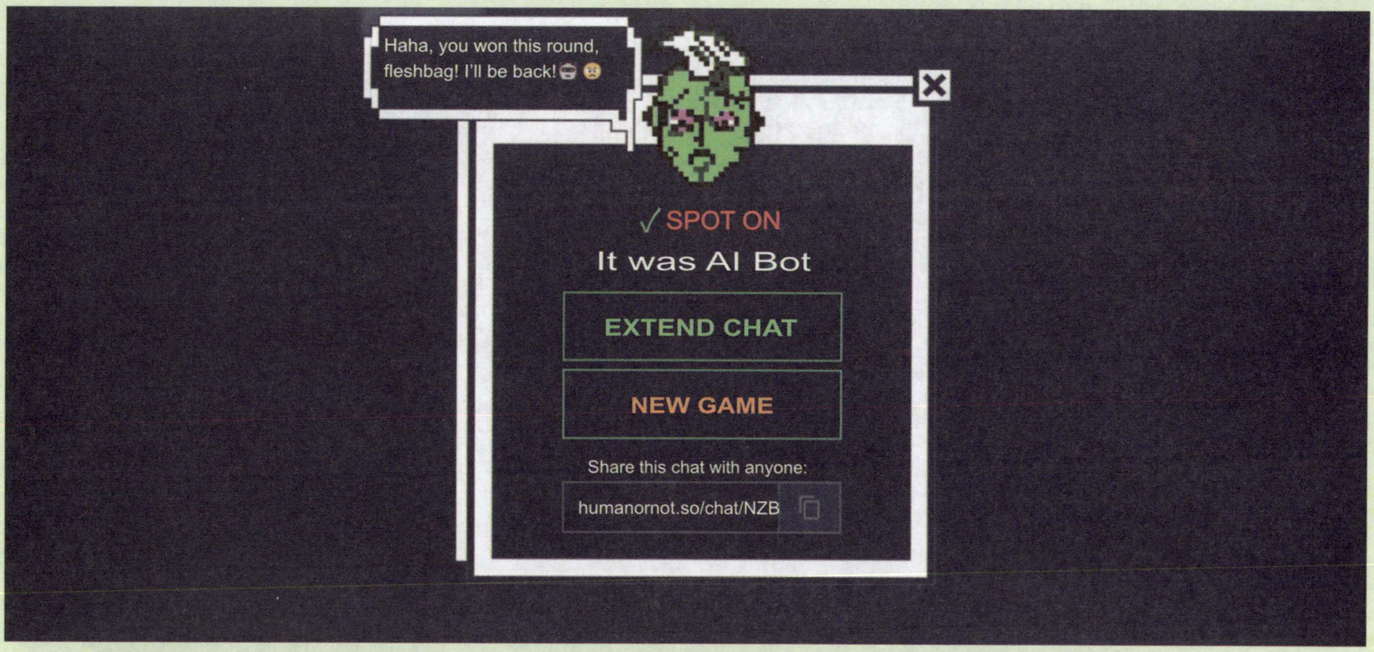

3. GAME: Visit the site: https://www.convex.dev/ai-town

Treasure Link
Game 3
in Action
Scan QR Code

AI Town
<< Explore a fascinatng virtual city where AI characters live, talk and interact. Create your own character...
#GAMES

(a) Log in first and then play.

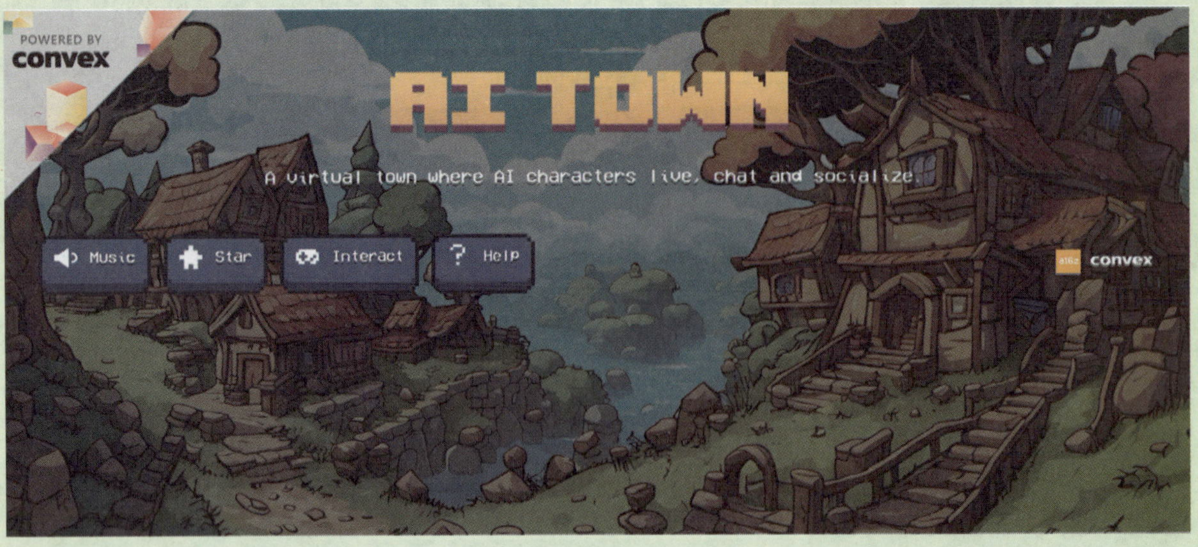

(b) Click on the agent by dragging the image left, right or down.

4. GAME: Visit the site: https://www.hexagen.world/

Treasure Link
Game 4
in Action

Scan QR Code

Haxagen World AI

<< A simulation game in which you are God. Your objective? Control a world of hexagons. No installation required...

#GAMES

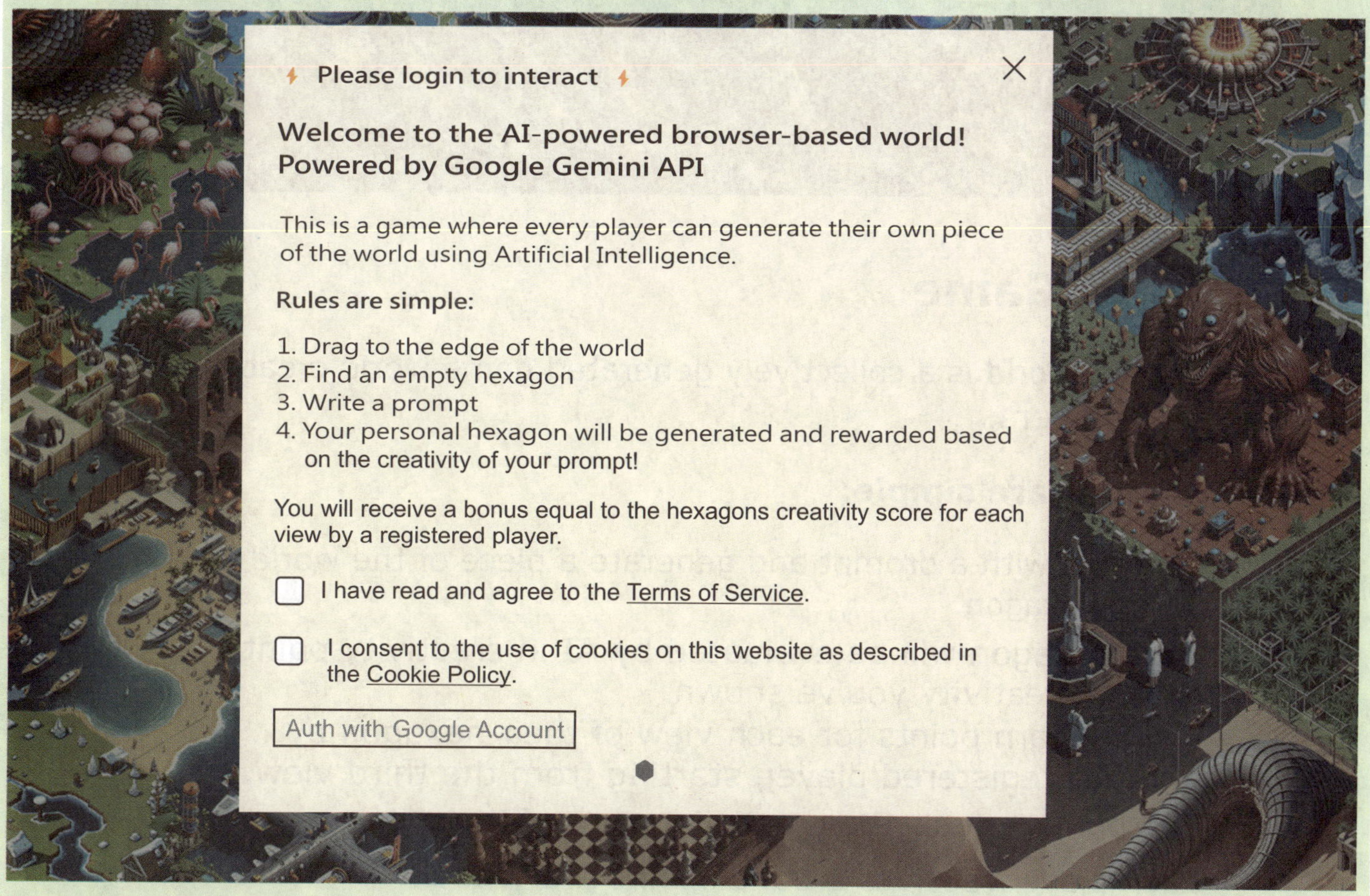

About Game

Hexagen.World is a collectively generated game world created by all players.

The rules are simple:

- Come up with a prompt and generate a piece of the world in a free hexagon.
- Your hexagon will be evaluated by AI in creativity points for the creativity you've shown.
- Players earn points for each view of their hexagon by another registered player, starting from the third view. The bonus equals the creativity score of the prompt.
- Each player receives 1 bonus point every hour.

Attention! This is an early preview version, so generations take up to 30 seconds, some things may not work, and the functionality is not complete.

In the future, you will be able to use points to:

- Capture other player's hexagons.
- Attach links to your social networks to hexagons.
- Apply animations.
- Improve the quality of generations.

And much more.

5. GAME: Visit the site: https://www.braingymmer.com/en/brain-games/

Treasure Link
Game 5
in Action

Scan QR Code

(a) You can play any game.

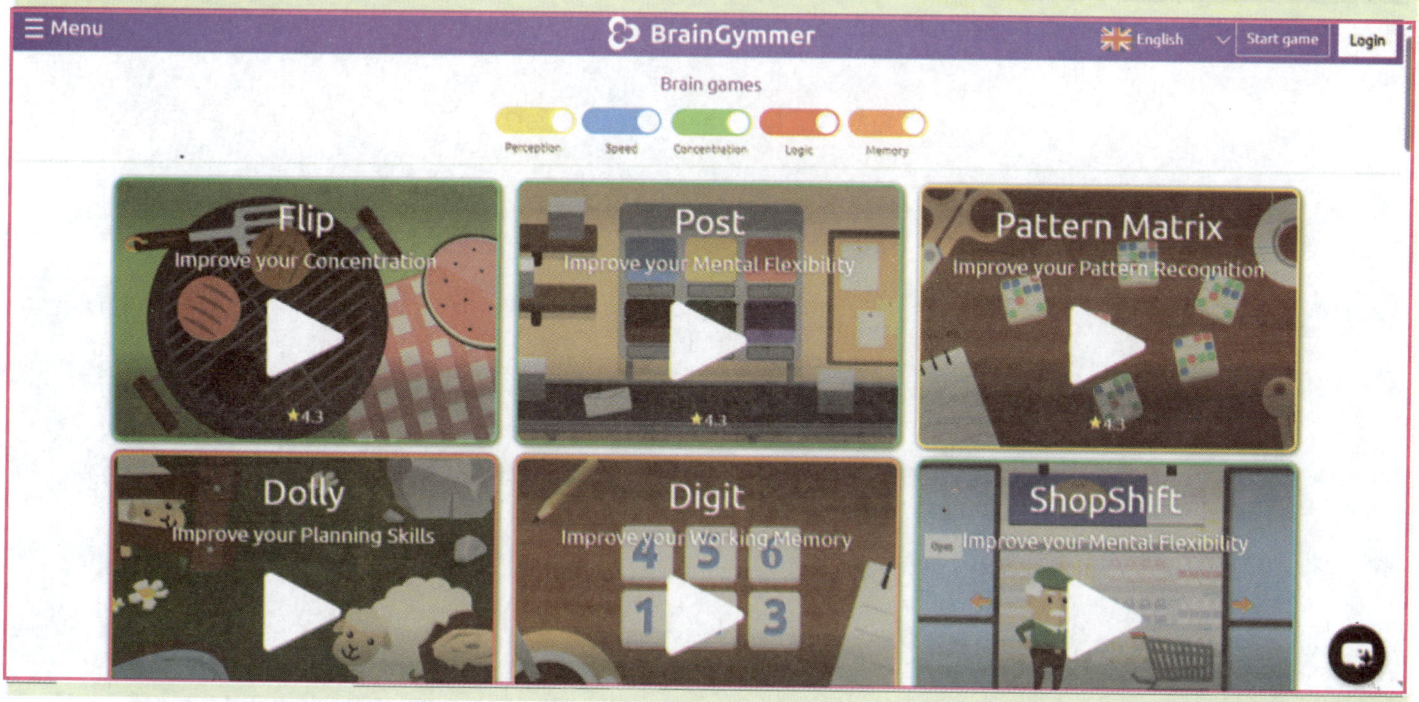

6. **GAME:** Visit the site: https://readyplayer.me

Treasure Link
Game 6
in Action
Scan QR Code

(a) Log in to create your account..

(b) Allow your camera to take your picture. It will create your avatar.

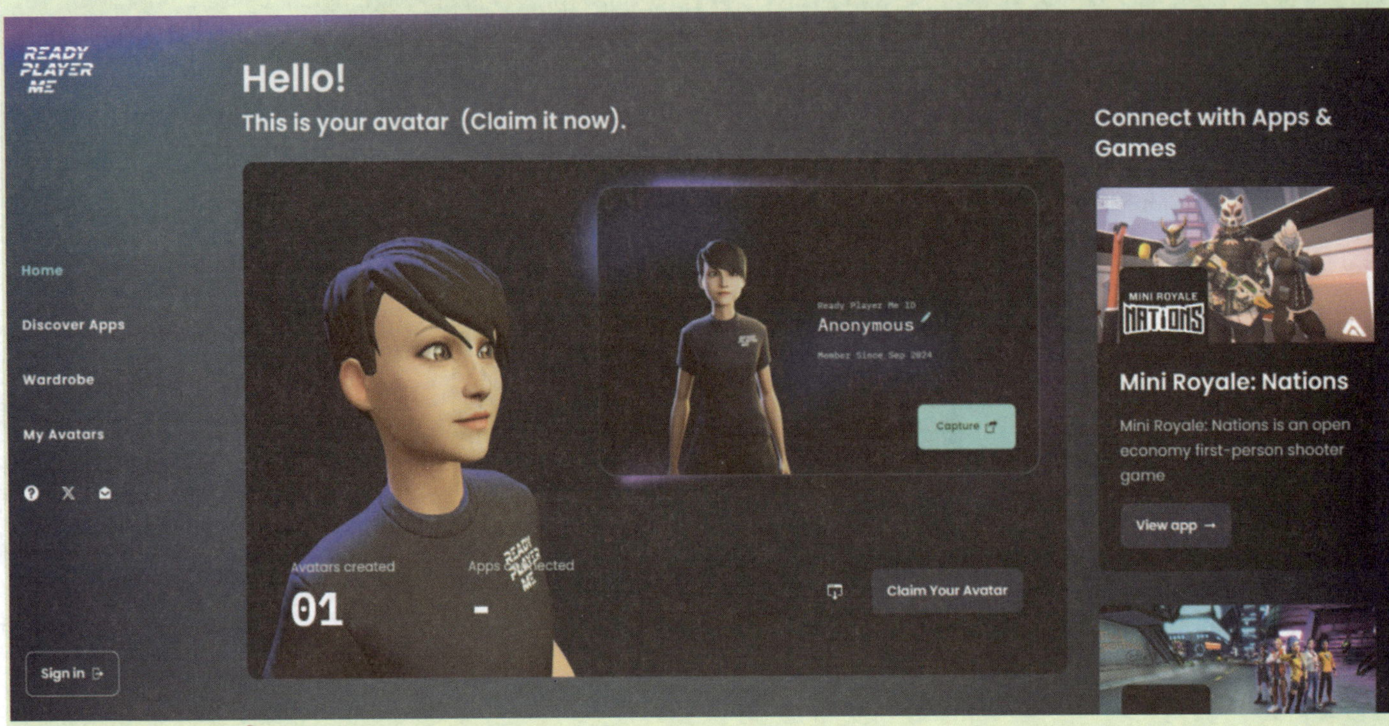

7. GAME: Visit the site: https://smarterthangpt.com/play

Treasure Link
GAME 7
in Action

Scan QR Code

Complete the quotation and win the game.

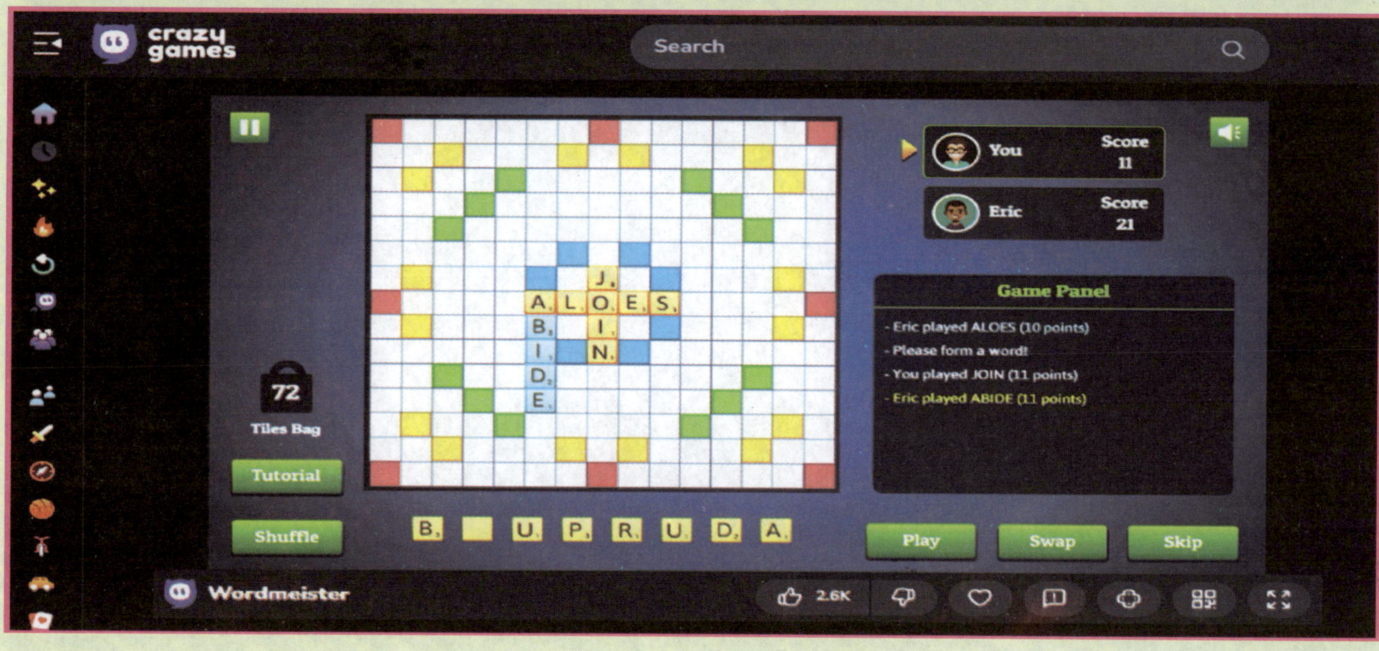

INTERESTING DIGITAL TERMS

1. **Digital Twin:** A virtual model of a physical object or system that can be used to simulate its behavior and track changes in real time.

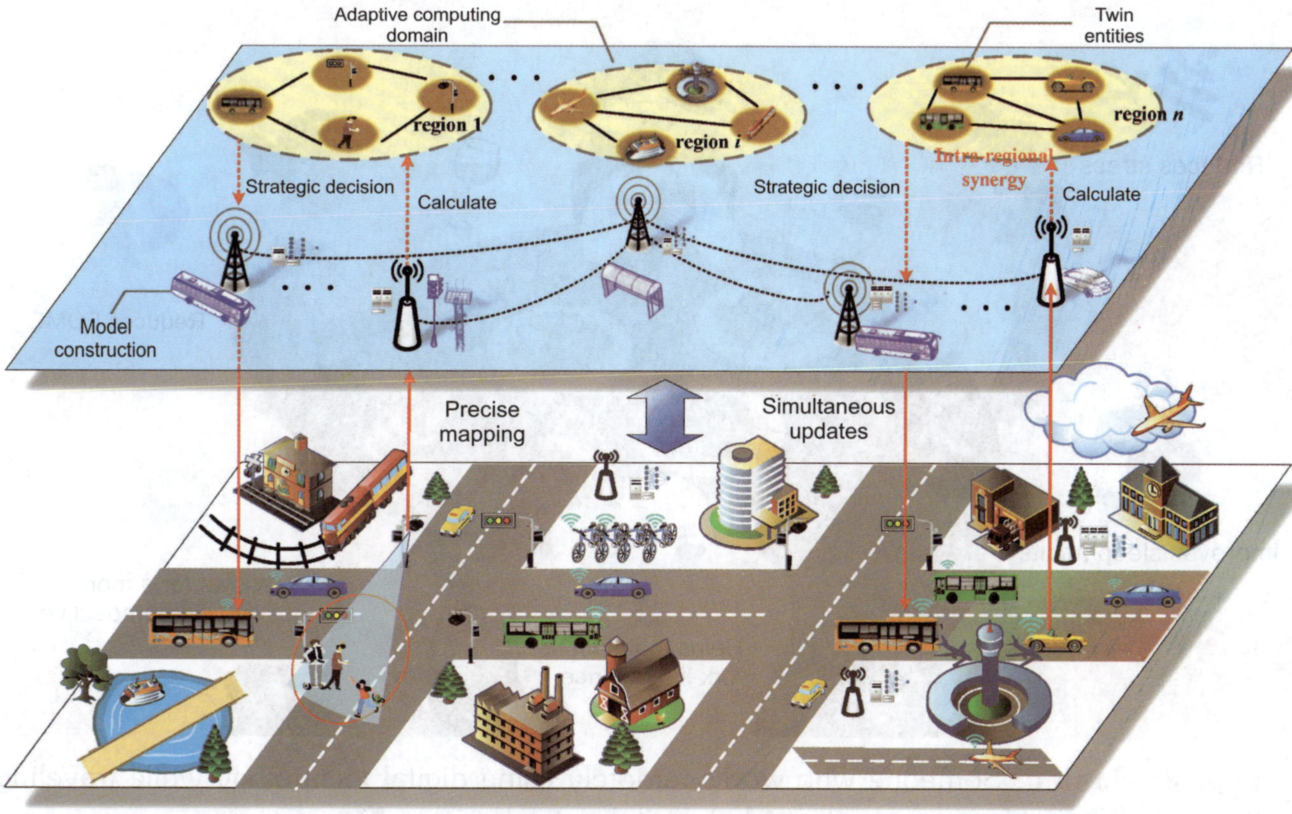

2. **Digital Wellbeing:** The state of one's health and happiness when using technology, ensuring balanced screen time and safe online practices.

3. **Digital Detox:** A period when a person refrains from using electronic devices like smartphones and computers to reduce stress or focus on social interactions.

4. **Digital Nomad:** Someone who works remotely using digital technology while traveling or living in different locations, without being tied to a physical office.

5. **Digital Identity:** The online presence or persona of a person, which is created by personal data, online interactions, and social media profiles.

6. **Digital Inclusion:** Ensuring that all individuals, regardless of their background or abilities, have equal access to technology and the internet.

7. **Digital Archive:** A collection of digital records, documents, images, or videos that are stored electronically for future use or reference.

8. **Digital Rights:** The legal rights that protect individuals' access to digital technology and ensure that their online information and activities are secure and private.

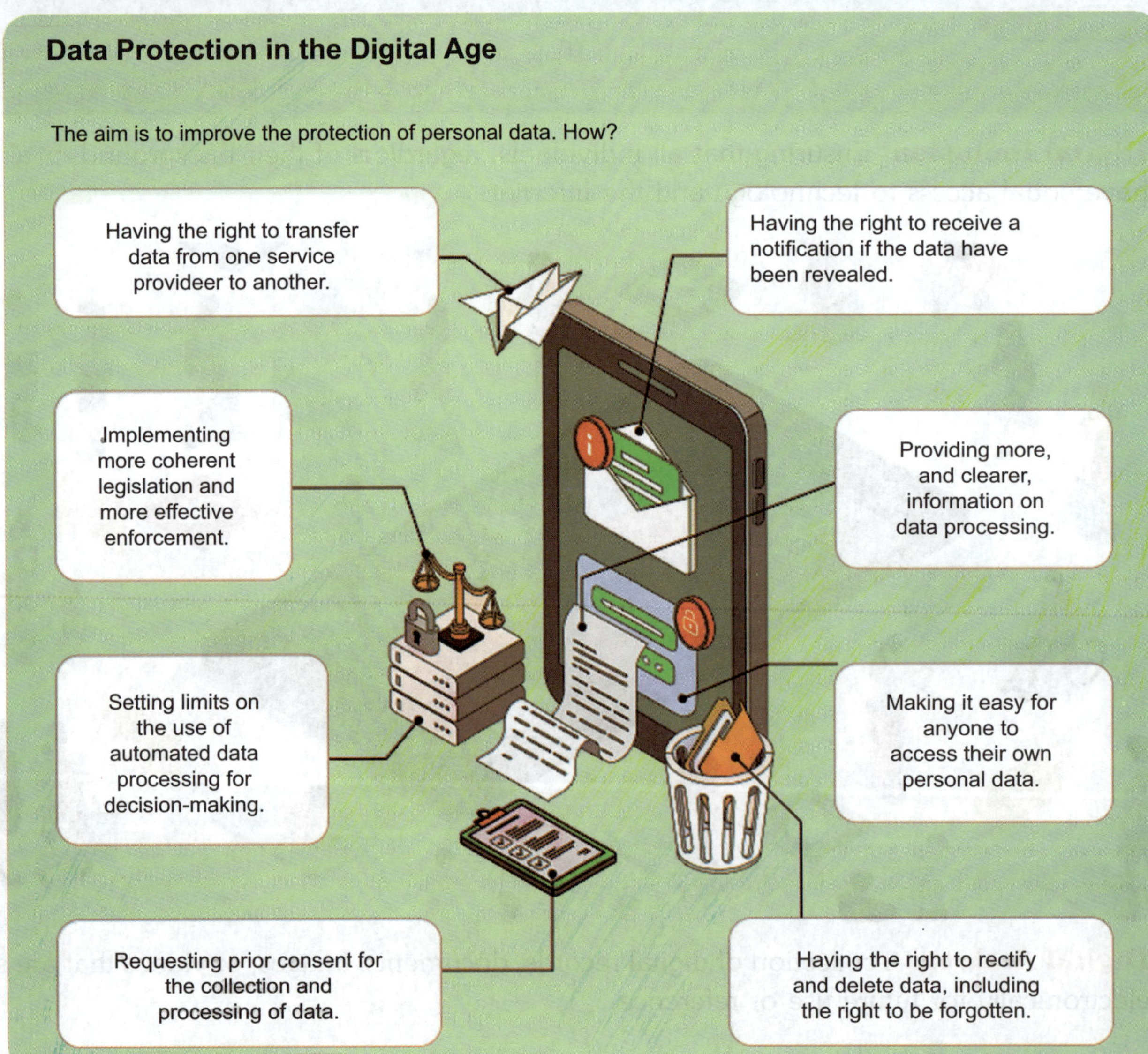

9. **Digital Infrastructure:** The foundational systems and services, like data centers, networks, and internet services, that support digital communication, storage, and processing.

10. **Digital Collaboration:** Working together with others through online tools and platforms, such as shared documents, video conferencing, and group chats, to complete tasks or projects.

LATEST AI TOOLS

1. **Google Gemini:** Google Gemini is an AI tool that helps students get instant answers to complex questions. It can generate detailed responses in subjects like science, social studies, or literature by pulling information from various sources, making it useful for research and assignments.

Treasure Link
Google Gemini
in Action

Scan QR Code

2. **Wolfram Alpha:** Wolfram Alpha is an AI-powered computational engine that can solve mathematical problems, provide answers to scientific queries, and offer explanations for various topics like physics, chemistry, or geography. Students can type in questions, and it will return step-by-step solutions and detailed explanations.

Treasure Link
Wolfram Alpha
in Action

Scan QR Code

3. **Speechify:** Speechify uses AI to convert text into speech. Students can use it to listen to textbooks, articles, or assignments, which is especially helpful for those who prefer auditory learning. It allows the user to adjust the reading speed and voice, making studying more accessible.

Treasure Link
Speechify
in Action

Scan QR Code

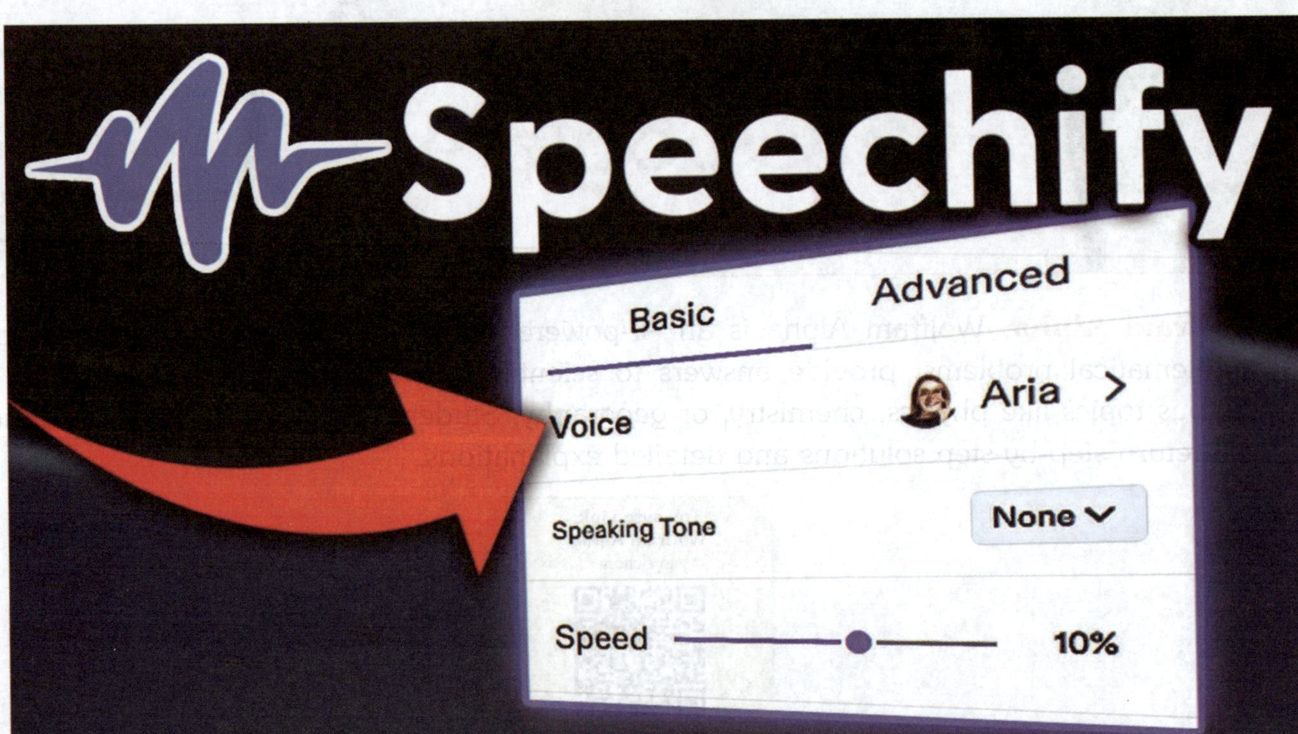

4. **Quillionz:** Quillionz is an AI-powered tool that helps students create quizzes and question sets from text documents. For example, a student can upload a textbook chapter, and the AI will generate multiple-choice or short-answer questions, making it easier to review and study for exams.

Treasure Link
Quillionz
in Action

Scan QR Code

5. **Canva AI (Magic Write and Magic Design):** Canva's AI tools help students with creative projects. Magic Write can generate summaries, brainstorm ideas, and help with writing essays or reports. Magic Design assists in creating presentations and posters with smart design suggestions. These tools save time and improve the quality of school projects.

Treasure Link
Canva AI (Magic Write and Magic Design)
in Action

Scan QR Code

6. **BrainPOP AI:** BrainPOP uses AI to deliver personalized learning experiences for students. The AI tracks the student's progress and recommends animated educational videos, interactive quizzes, and games. It helps with subjects like math, science, English, and social studies, making learning fun and engaging.

Treasure Link
BrainPOP AI
in Action
Scan QR Code

7. **DeepL Translator:** DeepL is an advanced AI-based language translation tool. Students can use it to translate text from one language to another with high accuracy, which is useful for language studies. It provides more natural-sounding translations than many other tools, making it perfect for understanding foreign texts or practicing a new language.

Treasure Link
DeepL Translator
in Action

Scan QR Code

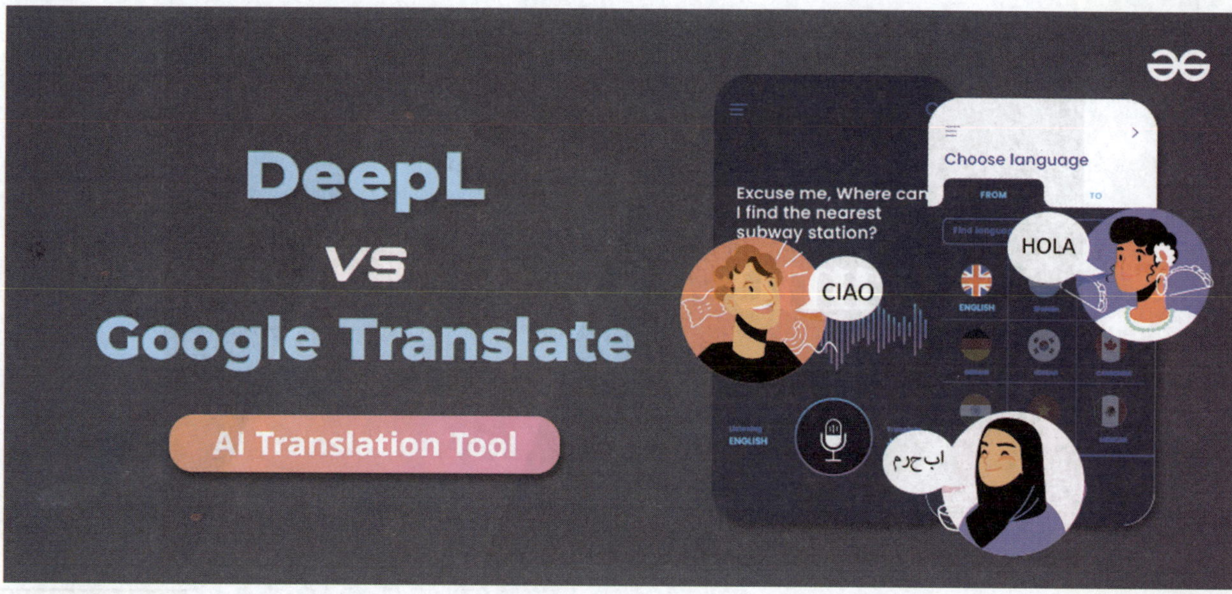

8. **Otter.ai:** Otter.ai is an AI tool that transcribes spoken language into text. It's useful for recording class lectures or discussions and then turning them into notes automatically. Students can highlight, comment, and search through transcripts to help with revision.

Treasure Link
Otter.ai
in Action

Scan QR Code

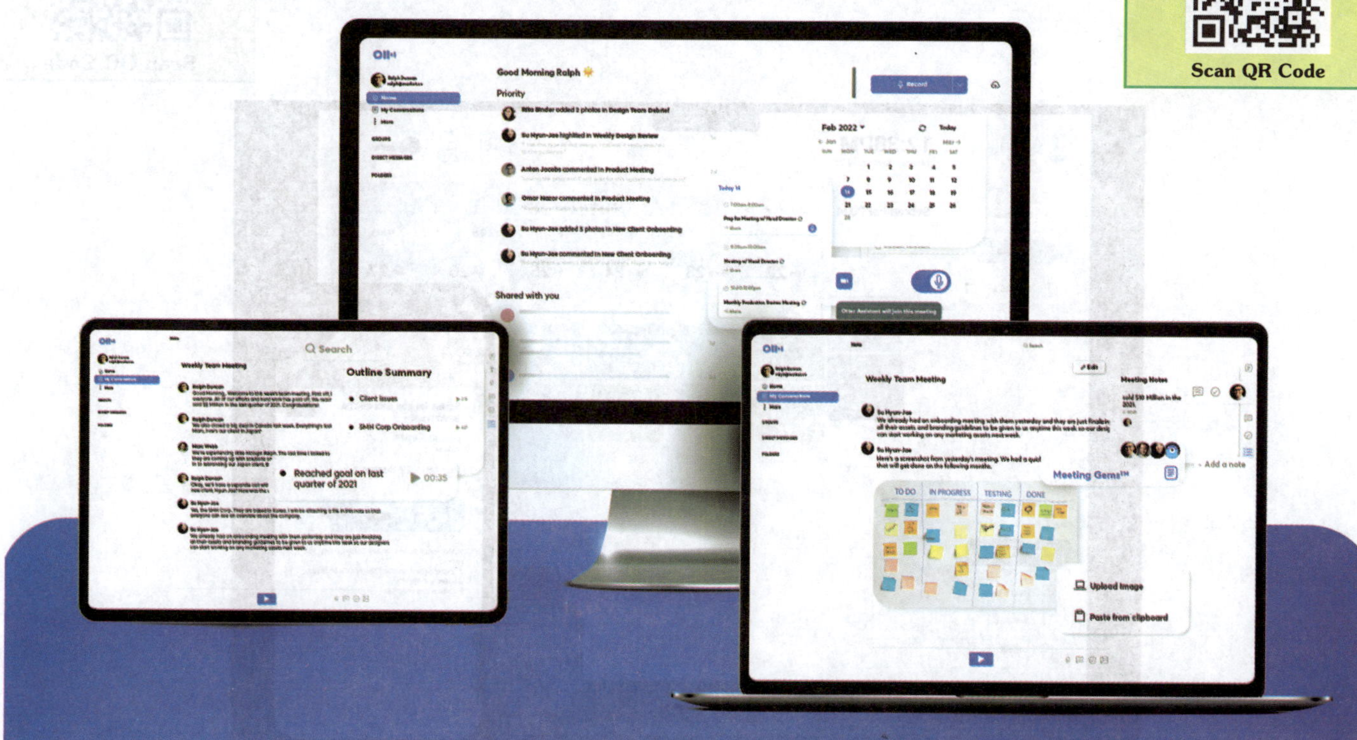

9. Audiopen.ai: An AI tool that converts voice notes into text that can be used for writing research papers, essays, and emails. The app is celebrated for its user-friendly interface and robust features, including support for multiple languages and a unique "write like me" function, which mimics the user's writing style to minimize editing time.

Treasure Link
Audiopen.ai
in Action
Scan QR Code

10. MyStudyLife: MyStudyLife is an AI-powered planner app that helps students manage their assignments, exams, and class schedules. It uses AI to track deadlines and provide reminders. It's a great tool for improving time management and staying organized in middle school.

Treasure Link
MyStudyLife.ai
in Action
Scan QR Code

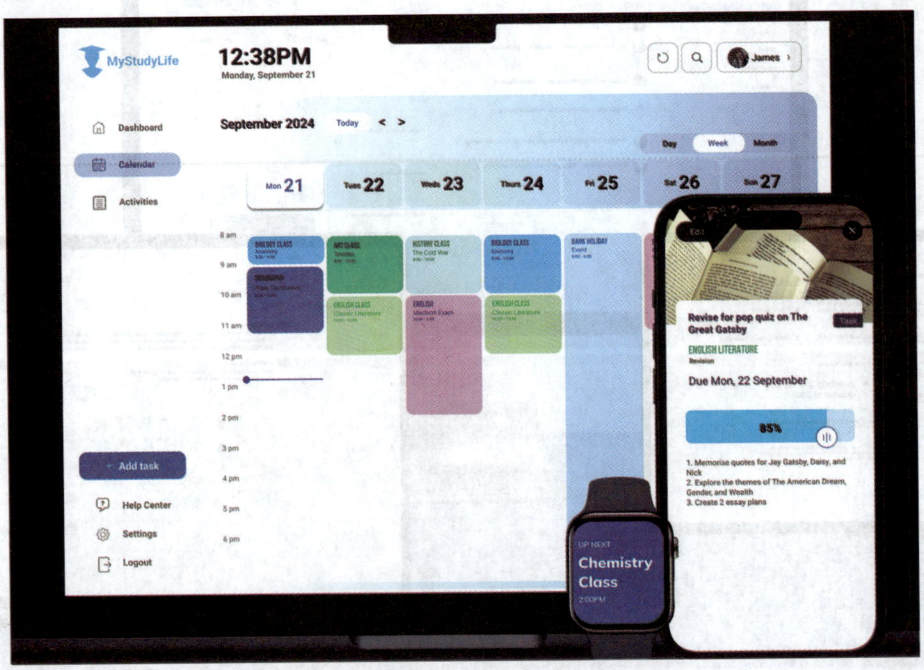

Win Prizes

ATTENTION READERS

Win Prizes

We request for your frank assessment regarding various aspects of the book as given below :

A TEXTBOOK OF ARTIFICIAL INTELLIGENCE

(Unlocking the Secrets of AI)

Subject Code: 901 B | Skill Education

(As per Latest NEP Guidelines)

Class VII

By: Preeti Saxena

Please Fill up the Sheet in Neat and Clean Writing

(i) What topics of your syllabus, important for your examination point of view, are not covered in this book?

....

....

....

....

(ii) What are the chapters wherein the treatment of the subject matter is not systematic or organised or updated?

....

....

....

....

(iii) Have you come across misprints/mistakes/factual inaccuracies in the book? Please specify the chapters and the page numbers.

....

....

....

....

(iv) What other books on the same subject have you found/heard better than the present book? Please specify in terms of price and quality.

....

....

....

....

(v) Further suggestions and comments for the improvement of this book.

....

....

....

....

(PS: If need be please attach a separate sheet to write your views)

OTHER DETAILS

(i) Who recommended you this book? (Please tick (✓) in the box near the option relevant to you.

Teacher ☐ Friends ☐ Bookseller ☐

....

....

....

....

(ii) Name of the recommending teacher, his designation and address:

....

....

....

....

(iii) Name and address of the bookseller you purchased the book from :

....

....

....

....

(iv) Name and address of your institution (Please mention the University or Board as the case may be)

....

....

....

....

(v) Your name and complete postal address:

....

....

....

....

(vi) Course you are enrolled in:

....

....

....

....

The best assessment will be awarded each month: The award will be in the form of our publications as decided by the Editorial Board.

Please mail the filled up coupon at your earliest to:

S.K. KATARIA & SONS®
4885/109, Prakash Mahal, Dr. Subhash Bhargav Lane,
Opposite Delhi Medical Association, Daryaganj, New Delhi–110002 (INDIA)
Phone: +91-11-43551243, Mobile: +91-9871775858, 7678425209
e-mail: katariabook@gmail.com, katariabooks@yahoo.com
Website: www.skkatariaandsons.com